Unbeaten Tracks in Japan

Isabella L. Bird

Nina Wegner

Mayumi Ushihara

装幀＝寄藤文平、吉田考宏

※本書の英文は、イザベラ・バードの著作を縮約し書き直したものです。
　地名の綴りなどは原作のままにしてあります。

日本奥地紀行
Unbeaten Tracks
in Japan

Isabella L. Bird
イザベラ・バード＝著

Nina Wegner
ニーナ・ウェグナー＝英文リライト

Mayumi Ushihara
牛原眞弓＝日本語訳

まえがき

　1878年4月、わたしは健康上の理由でイギリスを離れるよう勧められた。そこで、恵まれた気候と珍しい体験を求めて、日本へ旅することにした。日本のことがとても知りたかったし、きっとおもしろいだろうと思ったのだ。日本の気候にはがっかりしたが、この国は予想以上に興味深いところだった。

　本書は『日本についての本』ではない。むしろ、わたしの旅行記である。その目的は、この国のなかでも、外国人がほとんど見たことのない場所を旅することだ。日光から北への旅は、まさに未踏の奥地旅行だった。この地域へ足を踏み入れたヨーロッパ人は、わたしが初めてである。わたしは日本人のなかで暮らし、西洋の影響をまだ受けていない日本の生活様式を目にした。また、この旅行で蝦夷の先住民にも出会った。だから彼らのことや、その生活様式について、どのヨーロッパ人旅行者よりも詳しく記述できるはずである。

　記憶をたよりに旅行記を書くかわりに、旅行中に妹に書き送った手紙を読者の皆さんにお見せすることにしよう。わたしと同じ気持ちになって読んでもらうには、それが一番いいと思うからだ。これらの手紙を読めば、この未知の地域での旅の困難とともに、楽しさをも味わっていただけることだろう。

Preface

I was recommended to leave England for health reasons in April 1878. I decided to travel to Japan in search of good weather and unique experiences. I was very curious about Japan, and I was sure that I would find it very interesting. Although Japan's weather disappointed me, I found the country more interesting than I ever expected.

This is not a "book on Japan." Instead, it is a collection of stories about my travels. My aim was to travel through parts of the country that few foreigners had seen before. My travels north of Nikko were entirely on unbeaten tracks. I was the first European to go to these parts. I lived among the Japanese and saw their way of life, which was still untouched by European influence. On my travels, I even met the aborigines of Yezo. I believe I can give a better account of them and their lifestyle than any European traveler.

Instead of writing about my travels from memory, I am presenting the reader with the letters I wrote to my sister while traveling. I think this is the best way to put the reader in my shoes. As you read these letters, you'll experience the difficulties of travel in these unseen parts, as well as the enjoyment.

日光や江戸についてはすでに多くの著書があるため、本書では未踏の奥地にのみ注目している。また、北日本について書かれた文献はひとつもないので、わたしが学んだことはすべて、日本の地元住民から通訳を通して聞いたものである。アイヌの慣習や伝統について、アイヌたち自身が語ったままに読んでいただけるのだ。

　わたしは本書をできるだけ正確なものにしようと努めた。完璧ではないのは承知しているが、1,400マイル以上にわたる旅で目にした、そのままの日本を描こうと誠実に試みたつもりである。

　　　　　　　　　　　　　　　イザベラ・バード

Because much has already been written about Nikko and Yedo, this book will focus only on the unbeaten tracks. Since there is nothing written about Northern Japan, everything I learned came from Japanese locals, through an interpreter. You'll read about Aino customs and traditions as described by the Aino themselves.

I have worked hard to make this book as accurate as possible. I know it is not perfect, but it is my honest attempt to describe Japan as I saw it, on travels that covered more than 1,400 miles.

Isabella L. Bird

目次

まえがき 4

1章　横浜から江戸へ

横浜、オリエンタル・ホテルにて *18*
5月21日

横浜にて *24*
5月22日

江戸、英国公使館にて *26*
5月24日

江戸、英国公使館にて *30*
6月7日

江戸、英国公使館にて *36*
6月9日

2章　粕壁から日光へ

粕壁にて *44*
6月10日

日光、金谷邸にて *54*
6月15日

日光、金谷邸にて *58*
6月21日

CONTENTS

Preface 5

1. From Yokohama to Yedo

Oriental Hotel, Yokohama 19
May 21

Yokohama 25
May 22

H.B.M.'s Legation, Yedo 27
May 24

H.B.M.'s Legation, Yedo 31
June 7

H.B.M.'s Legation, Yedo 37
June 9

2. From Kasukabe to Nikko

Kasukabe 45
June 10

Kanaya's, Nikko 55
June 15

Kanaya's, Nikko 59
June 21

日光山、湯元、ヤシマ屋にて *62*
6月22日

日光、入町にて *66*
6月23日

藤原にて *72*
6月24日

3章　車峠から市野々へ

車峠にて *80*
6月30日

車峠にて *84*
6月30日

津川にて *88*
7月2日

新潟にて *90*
7月4日

新潟にて *94*
7月9日

市野々にて *98*
7月12日

4章　上山から神宮寺、黒石へ

上山にて *104*

金山にて *110*
7月16日

Yashimaya, Yumoto, Nikkozan Mountains ... *63*
June 22

Irimichi, Nikko *67*
June 23

Fujihara *73*
June 24

3. *From Kurumatoge to Ichinono*

Kurumatoge *81*
June 30

Kurumatoge *85*
June 30

Tsugawa *89*
July 2

Niigata *91*
July 4

Niigata *95*
July 9

Ichinono *99*
July 12

4. *From Kaminoyama to Shingoji, Kuroishi*

Kaminoyama *105*

Kanayama *111*
July 16

神宮寺にて	*114*
7月21日	
久保田にて	*120*
7月23日	
久保田にて	*124*
7月23日	
久保田にて	*128*
7月23日	
久保田にて	*132*
7月25日	
鶴形にて	*136*
7月27日	
大館にて	*140*
7月29日	
白沢にて	*144*
7月29日	
青森県、碇ヶ関にて	*148*
8月2日	
黒石にて	*154*
8月5日	
黒石にて	*158*
8月5日	
黒石にて	*162*

Shingoji *115*
July 21

Kubota *121*
July 23

Kubota *125*
July 23

Kubota *129*
July 23

Kubota *133*
July 25

Tsugurata *137*
July 27

Odate *141*
July 29

Shirasawa *145*
July 29

Ikarigaseki, Aomori-ken *149*
August 2

Kuroishi *155*
August 5

Kuroishi *159*
August 5

Kuroishi *163*

5章　函館から平取へ

蝦夷、函館にて *166*
1878年、8月

蝦夷、函館にて *170*
1878年、8月13日

蝦夷、函館にて *172*

蝦夷、じゅんさい沼にて *174*
8月17日

平取、アイヌの小屋にて *184*
8月23日

平取にて *194*
8月24日

蝦夷、佐瑠太にて *206*
8月27日

蝦夷、噴火湾、旧室蘭にて *208*
9月2日

函館にて *212*
9月12日

蝦夷、函館にて *216*
1878年、9月14日

江戸、英国公使館にて *218*
9月21日

江戸、英国公使館にて *220*
12月18日

5. From Hakodate to Biratori

Hakodate, Yezo *167*
August, 1878

Hakodate, Yezo *171*
August 13, 1878

Hakodate, Yezo *173*

Ginsainoma, Yezo *175*
August 17

Aino Hut, Biratori *185*
August 23

Biratori, Yezo *195*
August 24

Sarufuto, Yezo *207*
August 27

Old Mororan, Volcano Bay, Yezo *209*
September 2

Hakodate *213*
September 12

Hakodate, Yezo *217*
September 14, 1878

H.B.M.'s Legation, Yedo *219*
September 21

H.B.M.'s Legation, Yedo *221*
December 18

1章
横浜から江戸へ
(神奈川県)　　　(東京都)

From Yokohama to Yedo

横浜、オリエンタル・ホテルにて
5月21日

　雨の降る暗い海を18日間航海したあと、わたしたちの船はとうとう江戸湾に到着しました。どんよりと曇った日でしたが、日本の海岸はとてもきれいでした。森林に覆われたぎざぎざの山が水際からそびえ、**傾斜の急な屋根の家々が谷のあたりに群がっています**。イギリスの芝生のように青々とした棚田が、山腹の上のほうまで延びています。そして、いたるところに漁船がいます。ほんの5時間のうちに、何千もの漁船とすれ違いました。

　長いあいだ富士山を探して、やっと見ることができました。それは不意に、前方というより上のほうを見あげたとき、すばらしい幻覚のように**眼前に現れたのです**。空のように薄青く見え、高さは海抜13,080フィートもあります。そして、現れたときと同じように突然姿を消しました。日本人にとって聖なる山だというのも無理はありません。

　外国船の寄港が許されている唯一の場所、トリーティ岬【編注：本牧岬】に着きました。灰色で魅力のない横浜の町を見ていると、悲しくなってきました。この地には、知り合いがひとりもいないのです。でも、まもなく手漕ぎ船がわたしたちの蒸気船に近づいてきました。友人の親戚のギューリック博士が迎えにきて、手漕ぎ船で上陸するのを手伝ってくれたのです。

Oriental Hotel, Yokohama
May 21

富士山
Fujisan

After eighteen days of sailing on dark, rainy seas, our ship finally reached the Gulf of Yedo. The day was grey, but the coast of Japan is quite beautiful. Jagged, forested mountains rise from the water's edge, and **steep-roofed villages** cluster around the valleys. Rice terraces as green as English lawns run up mountainsides. There were fishing boats everywhere. We passed thousands in just five hours.

I looked for Fuji-san for a long time before I finally saw it. Suddenly, when I looked above rather than straight ahead, **it appeared before me** like a wonderful vision. It was pale blue like the sky and rose 13,080 feet above the sea. Then, as suddenly as it appeared, it vanished. No wonder it is a sacred mountain to the Japanese.

We arrived at Treaty Point, the only place where foreign ships **are allowed to dock**. As I looked at grey, unattractive Yokohama, I felt rather sad. I didn't know a single person in this land. But soon, little rowboats met our steamship. Dr. Gulick, a relative of some of my friends, met me and helped me onto shore by a rowboat.

日本の船はとてもうまく造られていて、腕のいい船頭が手で漕ぎます。船頭は丈の短い綿の上っ張りを着て、わらじをはき、青い鉢巻を額に巻いています。やせていて、肌は黄色く、伝説上の動物の入れ墨をしています。

　上陸して最初に気づいたことは、**みんな忙しそうに見える**ことでした。農民でさえ何か用事があるようです。どの人もとても小柄です。税関の建物では、西洋風の制服を着た小柄な職員が受け付けてくれました。彼らは注意深くて、ふるまいも丁寧でした——ニューヨークの税関職員よりも**ずっと礼儀正しいのです**！

　外に出ると、「クルマ」と呼ばれる人力車が50台くらいいました。これは日本特有の乗り物です。7年前に発明されたばかりですが、横浜にはすでに23,000台もいるのです。車夫は、ほかのどんな職工よりも多くの金を稼ぐことができるので、何千もの若者が車夫になろうと農家を出てきます。でも車夫はよく心臓や肺の病気になるので、長生きできないそうです。

人力車
A *Kuruma*

Japanese boats are well built and rowed by skilled boatmen. They wear short cotton jackets, straw sandals, and blue cloth tied around their heads. The boatmen are thin, their skin is yellow, and they are tattooed with mythical animals.

The first thing I noticed on land was **how busy everyone looked**. Even the peasants seem to have business to attend to. The people are very small. At the customs house, I was helped by tiny officials in European uniforms. They were careful and polite—**much better mannered** than the customs officials you meet in New York!

Outside, I saw about fifty *jinrikisha*, or *kuruma*. This vehicle is unique to Japan. It was invented only seven years ago, but already there are 23,000 in Yokohama. Men earn more money as a *kuruma* runner than almost any other kind of skilled labor. Thousands of young men leave their farms to become runners. I hear, however, that runners often get heart and lung disease and do not live long.

いろいろな人たち——商人、伝道師、おしゃれをした女たち、中国の貿易商、日本の農民——を見ながら、人力車で大通りを飛ぶように走っていくのは楽しいものです。車夫は汗をかきつつ疾走しながら、笑ったり叫んだりして、衝突しそうになるのをすれすれでかわしていきます。

　人力車に乗ってホテルへ向かいました。よく笑う小柄な車夫が、人の多い大通りを勢いよく運んでいきます。到着するとすぐに、フレーザー氏の事務所を探しに行きました。でも、これは大変でした。**通りには名前がないし、家の番号も順番に並んでいないからです。**

　見れば見るほど、横浜の町は好きになれません。ここでは何もかもが灰色なのです。フレーザー氏のところで、イギリス金貨を日本の札、つまり紙幣に両替しました。円の札束——50銭札、20銭札、10銭札——と、銅貨の包みを受けとりました。旅慣れた人なら、すぐにさまざまな金額がわかるのでしょうが、わたしにはまだよくわかりません。

　わたしは**本当の日本のなかへ入っていきたいのです**。領事のウィルキンソン氏によれば、日本では女がひとり旅をしてもまったく安全だそうです。ただし、蚤(のみ)と役立たずの馬が、日本の旅での一番大きな障害だと誰もが言っています。

It is amusing to see all kinds of people—merchants, missionaries, fashionable ladies, Chinese traders, Japanese peasants—flying along Main Street in a *kuruma*. The runners rush along, sweating as they laugh, shout, and barely avoid crashes.

I took a *kuruma* to my hotel. I was rushed along the busy Main Street by a laughing little man. As soon as I arrived, I went looking for Mr. Fraser's office. This was difficult, because **the streets have no names** and **the house numbers have no order**.

The more I see of Yokohama, the less I like it. Everything here is grey. At Mr. Fraser's, I exchanged my English gold into Japanese *satsu*, or paper money. I got bundles of yen—in 50, 20, and 10 *sen* notes—and some rolls of copper coins. Experienced travelers can recognize the different amounts instantly, but they are still confusing to me.

I want to **get away into real Japan**. Mr. Wilkinson, the consul, says Japan is perfectly safe for a lady traveling alone. Everyone agrees, however, that fleas and bad horses are the main difficulties of travel in Japan.

横浜にて
5月22日

　使用人と馬を見つけるため、人にいろいろ尋ねて一日が過ぎました。おかげで**新しい知り合いがたくさんできました**。ここの人たちは早寝早起きです。今日は午前中に13人の訪問客がありました。この町の女の人は、小さなポニーの馬車を別当(べっとう)と呼ばれる馬丁に引かせて、ひとりで出かけます。また、外国の商人たちが人力車をいつも玄関先に待たせているのにも気づきました。どんなに社会的地位が高くても——大使や大臣でさえも——ひとりで出かけられないということはないようです。

　今日の最後の訪問客、ハリー・パークス卿とその夫人は、親しみやすいご夫婦でした。ハリー卿が30年間も東洋に住んでいて、北京で監獄に入れられたこともあるとは**とても思えません**。ハリー・パークス夫妻がわたしの旅についてとても励ましてくれたので、使用人が見つかったらすぐにでも出発したいと思っています。

Yokohama
May 22

I spent the day looking for a servant and a horse, and asking many questions. **I made many new acquaintances.** People keep early hours here. Thirteen people visited me today before noon. The ladies in this town drive themselves in small pony carriages with grooms called *bettos*. I noticed that foreign merchants always keep a *kuruma* outside their door. It seems nobody—not even an ambassador or minister—is too high on the social ladder to travel in one.

My last visitors were Sir Harry and Lady Parkes, a friendly couple. **You would never guess** that Sir Harry has lived thirty years in the East, or that he was once a prisoner in Peking. Sir Harry and Lady Parkes were so encouraging about my travels that I'm eager to start as soon as I've found a servant.

江戸、
英国公使館にて
5月24日

　この手紙に「江戸」と記しましたが、日本の首都の新しい名前は東京といいます。「江戸」という名は、幕府という古い政府のときのもので、「東京」は維新政府がつけた名前です。新しい政府は、始まってからまだ10年しか経っていません。

　ここまでは列車で来ました。鉄道はイギリス人技術者が建造したもので、1872年に天皇の名によって開通しました。1等車と2等車は**がらがら**ですが、3等車には日本人がたくさん乗っていて、人力車での旅と同じように列車の旅を楽しんでいるようです。

　日本人は洋服を着るととても小柄に見えます。また、どの人も年齢がさっぱりわかりません。鉄道の職員たちが17歳か18歳だと思っていたところ、じつは25歳から40歳だと、あとでわかったほどです。

　今日はとてもすばらしい天気で、イギリスの6月の日のようでした。ただし、イギリスよりもかなり暑いです。ここではすべてが若々しく、新緑でいっぱいです。横浜のまわりの地域はとてもきれいで、森林で覆われた丘や、美しい谷があります。でも神奈川を過ぎたとたん、江戸の平野に入っていきます。この平野は南北に約90マイルあり、

H.B.M.'s Legation, Yedo
May 24

I have dated this letter "Yedo," but the new name of Japan's capital is Tokiyo. The name "Yedo" belongs to the old system of the Shogunate, while the name "Tokiyo" belongs to the Restoration. The new regime is only ten years old.

I journeyed here by train. The railway lines were built by English engineers and opened by the Mikado in 1872. While the first- and second-class cars are **quite empty**, the third-class cars are crowded with Japanese, who seem to enjoy train travel as much as traveling by *kuruma*.

The Japanese **look so small in European clothes**. It is also impossible to tell anybody's age. I thought the railway officials were about seventeen or eighteen. It turns out they are men from twenty-five to forty years old.

It was a beautiful day, like a June day in England, only hotter. Everything here is a young, fresh green. The land surrounding Yokohama is beautiful. There are wooded hills and pretty valleys. But once you pass Kanagawa, you enter the plains of Yedo. It is about 90 miles from north to south, and the clear blue waves of

東の海岸には、江戸湾の青く澄んだ波が広がっています。

　鉄道から見える土地はすべて念入りに耕され、ほとんどが**米作りのために水を引かれています**。見わたす風景のあちらこちらに村や寺があります。どこも居心地よく、美しく、そして明らかに勤勉な人たちの土地です。作物が整然と並んでいるあいだには、**雑草が1本も生えていないのです**。

　英国公使館の補佐官のデーヴィスが品川駅でわたしを出迎えて、公使館へ連れていってくれました。公使館の駐日公使はアーネスト・サトウ氏です。彼は日本史についての一流学者のひとりだと、日本人からも尊敬されています。

the Gulf of Yedo stretch along the eastern shore.

Every bit of land seen from the railroad is carefully farmed, and most of **it is irrigated for rice**. Villages and temples pop up here and there throughout the landscape. It is all homey and pretty, and clearly the land of a hardworking people. **Not a single weed can be seen** growing among the neat rows of crops.

Davies, an assistant at the British Legation, met me at the Shinagawa station and brought me to the Legation. The Japanese Secretary of Legation is Mr. Ernest Satow. He is considered by the Japanese to be one of the best scholars on Japanese history.

江戸、英国公使館にて
6月7日

　先週は横浜のヘプバーン博士夫妻を訪ねました。横浜には中国人が大勢います。小柄でやせていて、たいてい貧しそうな日本人たちとは、ずいぶん見かけが違います。日本には2,500人の中国人が住んでいて、そのうち1,100人が横浜に住んでいます。どこにいてもそうですが、中国移民はこの地でもたいへん役に立っているのです。中国人は背が高く、大柄で、ゆったりした絹の長服を着ています。頭の髪はほとんど剃り、**長い弁髪だけを腰まで垂らしています**。両替したり、列車の切符を買ったり、商人の事務所を訪ねたりすると、どこでも必ず中国人に会います。彼らにとって**人生の目的**は、お金を儲けることだけです。そのために中国人は熱心に働き、非常に成功しているのです。

　友人たちに手助けしてもらいながら、通訳を探しはじめました。多くの日本人が応募してきましたが、ほとんどの人がうまく英語を話せませんでした。それに、北日本や北海道へ旅をしたことのある人はひとりもいません。どうしてそんなところへ行きたいのかと、戸惑っているようでした。
　ひとりの応募者は、美しくて明るい色の西洋のスーツを着た若者でした。このように身なりのいい人を連れていけ

H.B.M.'s Legation, Yedo
June 7

I spent last week in Yokohama visiting Dr. and Mrs. Hepburn. I noticed there are many Chinese in Yokohama. They look quite different from the small, thin, usually poor-looking Japanese. There are 2,500 Chinese who live in Japan, and of these, 1,100 are in Yokohama. Here, as everywhere, Chinese immigrants are making themselves useful. The Chinese are tall and big, with flowing silk robes. Their heads are mostly shaved, **except a long braid that hangs to the waist**. You're sure to see a Chinese whenever you exchange money, buy a train ticket, or visit a merchant's office. **Their one goal in life** is to make money. For this, the Chinese work hard, and they are very successful.

With my friends' help, I began looking for an interpreter. Many Japanese came for the position, but most of them could not speak English well. None of them had traveled to Northern Japan or Hokkaido. They seemed confused as to why I would want to go to such places.

One applicant was a young man dressed in a beautiful light-colored European suit. I was afraid

ば、どこへ行っても高い値段をふっかけられるのではないかと、わたしは心配になりました。だから、ふたつ目の質問で彼の**英語力がお粗末だ**とわかったときは、ほっとしました。

ふたり目の応募者は、35歳の礼儀正しい男性でした。日本を旅行したイギリス人官吏のコックだった人です。この人には期待していたのですが、わたしが「主人もなしに」女ひとりで旅をしようとしていると知って、愕然としました。そのあとではもう、わたしを拒絶しているようでした。

平凡で丸顔の18歳の少年が、推薦状も持たずにいきなり現れたとき、わたしはがっかりしました。丈夫そうではありましたが、この子ほど頭の悪そうな日本人は見たことがありません。ところが彼は、アメリカ公使館で住みこみの事務員をしていたし、英語も書けるし、北日本を旅したこともあるし、料理もできるし、**奥地へ入る方法**も知っていると言うのです！　この完璧に聞こえる使用人には、なんの証明書もありませんでした。でもとりあえず、わたしはこの少年を月12ドルで雇うことにしたのです。

翌日、少年は時間どおりに現れて準備を整えました。手早く黙々と働き、ハリー・パークス卿夫妻にも深くお辞儀をして、このうえなく賢そうに見えました。少年の名前は伊藤といいます。きっと、これから3か月にわたって、彼についてもっとお知らせすることになるでしょう。

ここで知り合う人がみんな、わたしの旅行計画に興味を示しています。そしてどの人もアドバイスをくれるのですが、**そのほとんどが矛盾しています**。一番大事な問題だと

that traveling with such a well-dressed man would increase our prices everywhere we went. So, I was relieved when his **English skills broke down** after my second question.

The second applicant was a respectable man of thirty-five. He had been the cook of an English official who had traveled through Japan. I was hopeful about him, but he was horrified when he discovered that I was a woman traveling alone with "no master." He seemed to reject me after that.

I was feeling hopeless when a plain, round-faced boy of eighteen appeared out of nowhere with no recommendations. He looked strong, but he was the stupidest-looking Japanese I have ever seen. He said he'd lived at the American Legation, had been a clerk, could write English, had traveled through Northern Japan, could cook, and knew **how to get into the interior**! This perfect-sounding servant had no proof, but I hired him anyway for twelve dollars a month.

The next day, the boy appeared at the Legation on time and managed preparations. He works quickly and quietly, bows deeply to Sir Harry and Lady Parkes, and seems as smart as can be. His name is Ito, and I'm sure you will hear much more about him over the next three months.

My travel plans have interested all my acquaintances here. Everyone has advice to give, and **much of it is contradictory**. The issue that everyone says is

全員が口をそろえるのは、食べ物のことです。誰もが──牧師も、教授も、宣教師も、商人も──**食べ物のことをそれほど真剣に語るのです！** 残念なことに、パン、バター、肉、コーヒーのような西洋の食べ物はほとんどないようです。魚と野菜で作るひどくまずそうな日本料理に慣れることができなければ、米とお茶と卵でなんとかしのぐしかないだろうとのことです。

the most important is food. Everyone—ministers, professors, missionaries, merchants—**talks about food so seriously**! The sad truth is that European food, such as bread, butter, meat, and coffee, is rare. They say I will have to survive on rice, tea, and eggs, unless I can learn to eat the Japanese fish and vegetable dishes that sound so awful.

江戸、英国公使館にて
6月9日

　浅草寺についてお話ししましょう。これは観音（慈悲の女神）を祭る寺です。一般に、日本の寺はたいてい同じような外観をしています。あるのは屋根付きの門や、中庭、石段、寺を囲む縁側、巨大な屋根、そして仏像を安置した祭壇です。装飾物や仏像や祭壇などでいっぱいの寺もあれば、あっさりした質素な寺もあります。寺の建築には釘をほとんど使いません。建物を支える梁は、**ほぞ穴でみごとに組み合わされているのです。**

　浅草寺の正面の入口は、2階建ての二重屋根の門です。小さな店が参道に沿って並び、おもちゃからかんざしまで、なんでも売っています。門の近くにあるのは、数珠（じゅず）や、仏像、お守りなど、仏教で使う品物を売る店です。何百人もの人々が、ひっきりなしに門を通っていきます。門の両側には門を守るふたりの王、仁王の彫像が立っています。

　中庭に入ると、寺の本堂があります。この堂々とした建物は完全な木造建築です。寺は内陣（ないじん）と外陣（げじん）に分かれています。個人的に祈るためにお

石灯籠
Stone Lanterns

H.B.M.'s Legation, Yedo
June 9

I'll describe Asakusa Temple for you. It is dedicated to Kwan-non, the goddess of mercy. In general, most Japanese temples are similar in appearance. There is a roofed gate, a courtyard, a flight of stairs, a veranda that wraps around the temple, an enormous roof, and a shrine containing an image of Buddha. Some temples are full of ornaments, gods, shrines, and more, while other temples are simple and sparse. Very few nails are used in construction, because the support beams **are beautifully joined by mortises**.

The grand entrance of this temple is a two-storied, double-roofed gate (mon). Many little shops line its path, selling everything from toys to hairpins. Close to the gate are shops that sell rosaries, idols, amulet bags, and other items used in Buddhism. Hundreds of people pass through the gate every hour. On either side of the gate are the carved figures of the Ni-o, or two kings who guard the gates.

Next you enter the courtyard, then the temple itself. This imposing building is made entirely of wood. The temple is divided into inner and outer areas. Only those who have paid to pray privately are

金を払った人だけが、内陣に入れます。

外陣は活気に満ちていて、多くの人が行き来します。鳩が頭上を飛びかい、お経や、笑い声、太鼓の音、鐘の音など、さまざまな音がしてにぎやかです。**柱や壁には、髪の束などの供え物がぶらさがっています**。また、壮麗な守護神の木の彫刻もあり、鳩がしょっちゅうとまっています。

内陣の明かりは薄暗くなっています。この聖なる場所では、僧侶たちが静かに歩きながら、祈ったり、線香を灯したり、鐘を鳴らしたりしています。そして、高い祭壇の上に観音像があります。

僧侶
Buddhist Priests

もうひとつのお堂には、小さな紙つぶてがくっついた大きな像があります。その像を守る金網には、さらに何百もの紙つぶてがくっついています。人々は紙に願いごとを書いて、それを噛んで丸め、像に向かって吹き飛ばすのです。金網を通って像にくっついたら、いいしるしです。でも金網に引っかかったら、願いごとはかないません。病気を治す偉大な神、「びんずる」の像もあります。その顔は穏やかで威厳に満ちていますが、目、鼻、口、手、そして足も、**病人の手で撫でられてすり減っています**。何世紀ものあいだ、病人たちが癒しを求めて、この像の顔や手足を撫で、それから自分の体を撫でてきたのです。ひとりの少女が、目の悪いおばあさんをその像のところへ連れていくのを見かけました。少女は「びんずる」のまぶたを撫でてか

allowed into the inner temple.

The outer temple is full of activity, with many people coming and going. Pigeons fly above your head, and there is a great mix of sounds, including prayers, laughter, drums, and bells. **Offerings hang from the pillars and walls**, including braids of hair. There are also splendid wood carvings of angels, where the pigeons like to sit.

In the interior temple, the light is dimmer. Monks move silently through this holy place, praying, lighting incense, and ringing bells. On the high altar there is an image of Kwan-non.

In another shrine there is a large statue with little pellets of paper sticking to him. Hundreds more stick to the wire netting that protects him. People write their wishes on paper, chew it up, and spit it at the statue. If it passes through the wire and sticks, it's a good sign. But if it gets stuck in the netting, the prayer has not been heard. There is also a statue of Binzuru, a great medicine god. Although his face looks calm and dignified, his eyes, nose, mouth, hands, and feet **have been worn down by the hands of sick people**. For centuries, sick people have rubbed his face and limbs, then rubbed their own as a cure. I watched as a young girl led an old woman with bad eyes to the statue. The girl rubbed Binzuru's eyelids, then she gently stroked the eyelids of the old woman. I was

ら、おばあさんのまぶたをやさしく撫でていました。そのときわたしは、**この大きな寺は庶民のものであって、身分の高い人や金持ちだけのものではない**のだと改めて気づいたのです。

　大きな寺の境内では、さまざまな商売や娯楽が営まれています。茶屋では、きれいな娘さんたちが香りのよいお茶を勧めてきます。写真館、食べ物を売る屋台、それに歌や踊りの店もあります。ある店では、講談師が群衆に物語を聞かせていました。ピンク色の目と鼻を持つ神聖なアルビノのポニーが2頭いましたし、日本風のお辞儀をするようしつけられた猿回しの猿もいました。

　浅草は、日本でもっともおもしろい観光地のひとつです。帰り道で、**ロンドンにあるような赤い郵便車**のそばを通りました。また、西洋風の軍服を着た騎兵隊も見ました。海軍大臣の馬車のそばも通りましたが、これは6人の兵隊に守られていました。3週間前に内務大臣の大久保（利通）が政治的な理由で暗殺されてからは、警備が必要になったのです。天皇や、大臣、文官、警官、そして軍人も、みんな洋服を着ています。江戸は、古いものと新しいものが混ざった町だといえるでしょう。

　ここでは西洋風の家や家具がどんどん増えています。**これは悪趣味にしか思えません**。純粋に和風の装飾や家具をしつらえた伝統的な家にこそ、趣味のよさが見られます。

reminded that **this great temple is for the public**, not just for the noble and wealthy.

The large temple grounds contain many businesses and types of entertainment. At tea-houses, pretty girls invite you to drink fragrant tea. There are photograph galleries, food stalls, and booths for singing and dancing. In one booth, a professional story-teller was entertaining a crowd. There are two sacred Albino ponies with pink eyes and noses, and there are performing monkeys that have been taught to bow like the Japanese.

Asakusa is one of the most interesting sights in Japan. On our way back, we passed red mail carts, **like those in London**. We also saw a squadron of cavalry in European uniforms. We passed the carriage of the Minister of Marine, which was guarded by six soldiers. The guards have been required since the political assassination of Okubo, the Home Minister, three weeks ago. The Mikado, ministers, civil officials, police, and military all wear European clothes. Yedo is a city that mixes old and new things.

European-style houses and furniture are increasing here. **I find this to be in bad taste**. Good taste can be found in the traditional homes decorated and furnished purely in the Japanese style.

2章
粕壁から日光へ
(埼玉県) (栃木県)

From Kasukabe to Nikko

粕壁にて
6月10日

　長い旅がいよいよ始まったので、1日じゅう緊張しています！　泥棒に遭いはしないか、日本の礼儀作法を間違えてしまわないかなど、いろいろなことが心配なのです！　この計画をあきらめようかとも思いましたが、臆病者にはなりたくありません。

　荷造りは軽めにしました。わたしの荷物は1台の人力車に乗る分だけです。まずは折りたたみの椅子です。日本の**家は床以外にすわるところがない**ので、これが必要なのです。**しっかりした壁さえない**ので、もたれることもできないのですから。それから、人力車に乗っているときのための空気枕や、ゴム製の湯船、毛布、軽い支柱にキャンバス地のついた折りたたみのベッド。このベッドは組み立てれば2.5フィートの高さになるので、蚤から守ってくれるでしょう。食べ物については、もらったアドバイスはすべて無視して、牛肉エキスと、干しブドウ、チョコレート、ブランデーだけにしました。さらに着替えを少々と本を数冊、そのなかにはサトウ氏の英和辞典も入っています。

　日光にて、6月13日──ここは日本の楽園のひとつです！　日本にはこういうことわざがあります。「日光を見ずして結構と言うなかれ」（「結構」とは、「すばらしい」とか「美しい」という意味です）。でも、これについては、あとで書くことにしましょう。わたしたちは午前11時に公

Kasukabe
June 10

I have started my long journey, and I have been nervous all day! I'm afraid of being robbed, of breaking the rules of Japanese etiquette, of many things! I considered giving up this project, but I don't want to be a coward.

I packed lightly. All my things fit into one *kuruma*. I have a folding chair, which is necessary because **there is nothing to sit on except the floor** in a Japanese house. **They don't even have solid walls** for leaning against. I have an air pillow for *kuruma* travel, a rubber bath, a blanket, and a foldable canvas bed on light poles. It stands 2.5 feet high, protecting me from fleas. For food, I've rejected all advice and simply brought some beef extract, raisins, chocolate, and brandy. I have a few changes of clothes and several books, including Mr. Satow's Anglo-Japanese Dictionary.

Nikko, June 13—This is one of Japan's paradises! There is a saying in Japan, "If you haven't been to Nikko, then you cannot use the word *kek'ko*" (meaning "splendid" or "beautiful"). But I'll write about that later. We left the Legation at 11 a.m. and

使館を後にし、午後5時に粕壁へ着きました。人力車の車夫たちは、かなりの速さで23マイルを走りました。**彼らの髪型は見苦しいものです。**頭の前とてっぺんの髪を剃り、両側と後ろの長い髪を結んで、前を指すように頭の上に載せています。以前は武士がこのような髪型をしていましたが、いまでは身分の低い階級の人たちの髪型になっているのです。

江戸を出ると、家はほとんどなくなっていきました。店や茶屋がたまにあって、魚の干物、漬物、餅、干し柿、雨笠、わらじなどを売っていました。このことを書かなければならないでしょうか?──ここでは人も家も貧しくて、みすぼらしいようすでした。

江戸平野は田んぼだらけで、何百という男女が水田の中で働いています。日本には主に約9種類の米があり、どの米を育てるにも、泥と、水と、汚れる仕事が必要です。**米は日本の財産であり、収入は米の量で示されます。**

reached Kasukabe at 5 p.m. My *kuruma* runners ran the twenty-three miles at a good pace. **They wear their hair in an ugly fashion**. The front and top of the head is shaved. The long hair from the sides and back are tied and lay on top of the head, pointing forward. The samurai used to wear their hair like this, but now it's the style of the lower classes.

Outside of Yedo, there were fewer houses. Some were shops or tea-houses, selling dried fish, pickles, *mochi*, dried persimmons, rain hats, and straw shoes. Must I write it?—both the people and houses here looked poor and shabby.

The plain of Yedo is full of rice fields, with hundreds of men and women working in the water. There are about nine leading varieties of rice in Japan, all of which require mud, water, and dirty work. **Rice is the wealth of Japan** and its revenues are measured in rice.

元気よく数マイル走ったあと、車夫たちは茶屋で一服しました。彼らは足を洗うと、ごはん、漬物、塩漬けの魚、みそ汁を食べました。娘さんが小さな急須にお茶をいれて持ってきてくれました。日本茶はとてもいい香りでおいしいのです。**いつ飲んでも、清々しい気分になります。**ミルクと砂糖は入れません。

　その夜は、粕壁にある大きくて混んだ宿屋に泊まりました。古い家で、台所には使用人が30人くらいいました。わたしは2階の部屋に泊まりましたが、畳敷きの床以外まさに空っぽでした。日本の敷物（畳）は、イギリスの最高級のカーペットと同じくらい整然として上品です。無神経な外国人が汚れた靴のまま畳の上にあがると、日本人は気分を害します。でも残念なことに、**畳は蚤にとっても最高の住み家になりやすいのです。**

茶屋
Road-Side Tea-House

After running cheerily for several miles, my men stopped at a tea-house. They washed their feet and ate rice, pickles, salt fish, and soup. A girl brought me some tea in a tiny teapot. Japanese tea has a delicious aroma and flavor. **It is refreshing at all times**. Milk and sugar are not used.

We spent the night at a large, crowded *yadoya* in Kasukabe. It is an old house, with about thirty servants in the *daidokoro*. I took a room upstairs that was completely empty except for the matted floor. Japanese mats (*tatami*) are as neat and refined as the finest English carpet. It upsets the Japanese to see thoughtless foreigners step on them with dirty shoes. But, unfortunately, ***tatami* can be a perfect home for fleas**.

わたしは眠ろうとしましたが、ふすまを開けてわたしを見ようとする人たちに邪魔されて眠れませんでした。そこらじゅうで物音がしました。隣の部屋では三味線を弾く人や、お経を唱える人がいるし、家じゅうで話し声がするし、火の用心の人が一晩じゅう拍子木を打ち鳴らしていました。そのうえ、ほぼ真夜中に伊藤がやってきて、ふたりの警官がわたしに会いたがっていると言うではありませんか！　わたしは怖くなりましたが、警官たちの態度はとても丁重だったので、すぐに安心しました。彼らはわたしのパスポートを見たかっただけなのです。わたしの緊張も時間とともに和らぐでしょう。そのうち、ここでの暮らしに慣れると思います。

　朝になると、日光への旅を続けました。ふたつの川を渡ると、稲田は小麦畑に変わり、そのそばに豆や、大根や、キュウリが植えられていました。**ひとつの作物を収穫するとすぐ、ほかの作物をその場所に植えるのです。**土地は1年に2回、ときには3回も作物を産み出します。雑草は1本も見当たらず、国そのものがよく手入れされた庭園のようです。

　旅を続けるうちに、風景がますます美しくなってきました。居心地のよさそうな農村が、濃緑の森のなかに見え隠れします。雪をかぶった山々が、緑なす丘の上に顔をのぞかせています。丘の頂上にはたいてい神社があり、白とピンクのツツジがいたるところに咲いていました。日光に近づくにつれ、日本は本当に美しいと思うようになりました。

　大谷橋（だいやばし）を渡ったあと、泊まる予定の家に着きました。宿の主人の金谷（かなや）氏は、とても感じのいい人です。でも、車夫

I tried to go to sleep, but I was distracted by people opening the *fusuma* to look at me. There were noises all around: someone in the next room played a *samisen*, someone recited Buddhist prayers, the house was full of talking, and the fire watchman clapped his two pieces of wood together all night. Then, near midnight, Ito came and said two policemen wanted to see me! This frightened me but the policemen were so respectful that I immediately felt better. They simply wanted to see my passport. I know my nervousness will go away with time. Soon I will get used to life here.

In the morning, we continued to Nikko. After we crossed two rivers, the rice fields gave way to wheat fields, along with beans, *daikon*, and cucumbers. **As soon as one crop is harvested, another takes its place**. The land can produce two or even three crops in one year. I haven't seen a single weed, and the whole country is like a well-kept garden.

As we journeyed, the landscape became more beautiful. Comfortable farming villages nestled among dark green forests. Snow-covered mountains peeked over the wooded hills. Shinto shrines crowned many hilltops, and white and pink azaleas blossomed everywhere. As we neared Nikko, I felt that Japan is truly beautiful.

After crossing the Daiya Bridge, we arrived at the house where I will stay. Kanaya, the landlord, is

たちと別れるのは悲しいことでした。彼らはとても親切にしてくれたからです。しょっちゅうわたしの服のほこりを払い、枕の空気を入れ、花を持ってきてくれました。ついさっきも山へ行って、お別れの挨拶のためにツツジを取ってきてくれたのです。わたしが出会った車夫はどの人も、このうえなく礼儀をわきまえた人たちです。

車夫
Mr. *Kuruma*-Runner

a very pleasant man. But I was sad to part with my *kuruma* runners. They have been very kind to me. They always dusted my dress, filled my pillow with air, and brought me flowers. Just now, they went to the mountains and brought me some azaleas to wish me goodbye. Every *kuruma* runner I've met is extremely polite.

日光、金谷邸にて
6月15日

　わたしが泊まっている家は、まるで日本風の天国です。水の流れる音と、鳥のさえずりに囲まれています。この家は2階建てで、庭にはボタン、アヤメ、ツツジが咲いているのです。家の真後ろに山がそびえ、その脇からきれいな小川が流れ落ちてきます。小川は家の下を通り、魚のいる池を過ぎて、やがて飲み水になります。道の向こうに入町(いりまち)村があり、そのすぐ先に大谷川(だいやがわ)が流れています。

　家の縁側はよく磨かれていて、美しい景色が見渡せます。畳があまりに上等で真っ白なので、**ストッキングをはいていても歩くのが怖いほどです**。部屋の前には障子が並び、日中は開け放たれています。ふすまは空色の紙に金を吹きつけたものです。部屋の奥には、ふたつの床の間があります。そのひとつには桜の花が咲く枝の絵が掛かっていて、部屋にいきいきとした美しさを振りまいています。もうひとつの床の間に置かれているのは、古めかしい飾り棚です。**部屋がこれほどすばらしくなければいいのに、と思うくらいです**。というのも、インクをこぼしはしないか、障子を破りはしないか、畳をへこませはしないかと、ずっとはらはらしているからです。また、階下の部屋も同じように美しいのです。

Kanaya's, Nikko
June 15

My house is a Japanese paradise. We are surrounded by the sound of water and the twitter of birds. The house is two-storied with a garden of blooming peonies, irises, and azaleas. A mountain rises just behind the house, and a clear stream tumbles down its side. It passes under the house and through a fish pond, supplying drinking water. Irimichi Village is on the other side of the road, with the Daiya River just beyond.

The verandas of the house are polished and provide beautiful views. The *tatami* mats are so fine and white that **I'm afraid to walk on them, even in my stockings**. The front of my room is lined with *shoji*, and they are slid back during the day. The *fusuma* are sky-blue paper splashed with gold. At the end of my room are two tokonoma. A painting of a blossoming cherry branch hangs in one, filling the room with freshness and beauty. In the other is an antique cabinet. **I almost wish that the rooms were a little less exquisite**, because I'm constantly afraid of spilling ink, tearing the paper windows, or denting the mats. The rooms downstairs are equally beautiful.

金谷氏はこの村の村長で、とても聡明で教養のある人です。そして彼の妹は、これまでに会った日本女性のなかで一番やさしくて上品な女の人です。妖精のように軽やかに家のなかを行き来し、音楽を奏でるような声で話します。金谷氏は最近部屋を外国人に貸すようになったばかりだそうで、心からもてなしてくれます。でも趣味がとてもいいので、自分の美しい家を「**西洋化**」するようなことはしていません。個人の家に泊まって、日本の家庭生活を目にするのは、じつに興味深いものです。

金谷邸
Kanaya's House

Kanaya is the chief man in the village. He is very intelligent and well-educated. His sister is the sweetest and most graceful Japanese woman I have ever seen. She floats through the house like a fairy, and her voice is musical. Kanaya recently started renting his rooms to foreigners, and he is very eager to please. But his good taste prevents him from "**Europeanizing**" his beautiful home. It is very interesting to live in a private house and to see Japanese domestic life.

日光、金谷邸にて
6月21日

　わたしは日光に9日間滞在したので、いまでは「結構！」と言うことができますね。日光とは「太陽の輝き」という意味で、日本の詩にはその美しさを称えるものがたくさんあります。ふたりの偉大な将軍を祭る神社が、どのような魅力に取り囲まれているか、その一部をご紹介しましょう——雪をかぶった男体山（なんたい）、壮大な森、静かな湖、華厳の滝（けごん）、中禅寺湖、霧降ノ滝（きりふり）の鮮やかな美しさ、そして大いなる大谷川です。

　徳川幕府の第2代将軍が、父の家康をこの地に葬りました。これは**壮麗なお墓**なのです。その葬儀は、勅使や大名や僧たちが居並ぶ立派なものだったということです。

　神社の境内へ入るもっとも大きな参道は、赤橋を通る道です。ここから広い道を歩いていくと、高さ27フィート6インチのみごとな鳥居が立っています。そのあとに、118基もの堂々とした青銅の灯籠が並び、青銅の鐘、燭台など、朝鮮の王のように身分の高い人からの贈り物も置かれています。

　最初の中庭に入っていくと、**その荘厳さに圧倒されます**。建物も、設備も、それらの配置も、日本独特のものです。仁王門からこの中庭を眺めると、まるで夢のなかを見ているようです。ここから有名な美しい庭を通って歩いて

Kanaya's, Nikko
June 21

I've been at Nikko for nine days, so I can now say "*kek'ko!*" Nikko means "sunny splendor," and many Japanese poems praise its beauty. Here are just some of the attractions that surround the shrines of the two greatest Shoguns: the snow-covered Nantaizan, magnificent forests, serene lakes, the waterfalls of Kegon, Chiuzenjii Lake, the bright beauty of Kiri Furi falls, and the grand Daiyagawa.

The second Shogun of the Tokugawa dynasty buried his father, Iyeyasu, here. It is **a glorious resting place**, and I am told the funeral was splendid with an imperial envoy, *daimyo* and priests.

The grandest approach to the temple complex is by the Red Bridge. From here, you walk up a broad road to a fine *torii* that stands 27 feet 6 inches high. After this come 118 magnificent bronze lanterns, as well as a bronze bell, candelabra, and other gifts from such dignitaries as the king of Corea.

Walking into the first courtyard, **you feel overwhelmed by its magnificence**. The buildings, the arrangements, the layout is uniquely Japanese. Glimpsing this court from Ni-o gate is like seeing

いくと、感嘆の連続でへとへとになりそうでした！　なかでも陽明門のことを思わずにはいられません——麒麟の豪華な彫刻を思い出すたびに、感動で胸がいっぱいになるのです！

　家康の遺骨は丘の上の墓のなかで、自然に囲まれて眠っています。墓、石の回廊、石の階段など、石工技術のすばらしさに感銘を受けました。**すべてがモルタルもセメントも使わずに造られている**のに、260年たってもまだ完璧な姿をとどめているのです。

　すぐそばの家光を祭る寺は、それほど荘厳ではありませんが、やはり同じくらい魅力的です。これらの神社や寺へは何度も足を運びましたが、ふと振り返れば、金箔の扉、黒や赤の漆、巨大な鐘の光景が頭のなかいっぱいに広がります。そして香の匂いを感じ、非常に美しい孔雀や、コウノトリ、蓮、松、牡丹、竹の絵が目に浮かぶのです。また、仏塔や青銅の灯籠、木の彫刻、頭を剃った僧たち、神官たちを思い出します。そして、杉林の木陰を明るく照らすツツジの花に思いを馳せるのです。

something in a dream. From here, I walked through numerous beautiful courts until I was almost exhausted from admiration! I cannot stop thinking about Yomei gate—remembering its richly carved *kirin* continues to fill me with wonder!

Iyeyasu's remains rest in an urn on top of a hill, surrounded by nature. I was impressed by the masonry of the tomb, the stone gallery, and the stone stairs. **All were built without mortar or cement**, and yet they still look perfect 260 years later.

The nearby temples of Iyemitsu are less magnificent but just as fascinating. When I think back on my multiple visits to these shrines and temples, my head fills with visions of gold-gilded doors, black and red lacquer, and enormous bells. I smell incense and see exquisitely painted peacocks, storks, lotuses, pines, peonies, and bamboo. I remember pagodas and bronze lanterns, wood carvings, bald priests, and Shinto attendants. I think of azaleas brightening the shade of cedar forests.

日光山、湯元、ヤシマ屋にて

6月22日

　今日は馬に乗って湯元へ行きました。日本の荷馬に乗るのは初めてです——とてもおもしろい経験でした。日本の馬についてはひどい話ばかり聞いていましたし、実際に乗るまで、わたしにとっては麒麟のような伝説上の動物だったのです。でもありがたいことに、振り落されはしませんでした。雌のほうがおとなしいので、この地域では雌馬しか使わないのです。

荷馬
Japanese Pack-Horse

Yashimaya, Yumoto, Nikkozan Mountains
June 22

Today I rode to Yumoto on horseback. It was my first time on a Japanese pack-horse—**an interesting experiment**. I'd heard terrible things about Japanese horses, and before I rode one they were as mythical to me as the *kirin*. Thankfully, I did not get kicked off. Only mares are used in this district because they are gentler.

馬子という、馬の世話をする男がわらじを馬の足に結びつけ、荷物をすべて馬の背に載せます。**これにはかなりの技術**が必要で、バランスをとらなければなりません。馬に乗るのにも、うまくバランスをとる必要があります。

　今日の旅の終わりには、汚れて疲れきった人間より、妖精のほうが似合いそうな美しい宿屋に着きました。ふすまは、いい香りのする木で作られていて、縁側はよく磨かれた松の木です。笑顔の少女が、アーモンドのような風味の、梅の花入りのお茶を運んできてくれました。

　夜には、村や浴場を見て回りました。湯元は標高が4,000フィート以上で、とても寒いところです。村には人がいっぱいいて、4つの浴場はとても込んでいました。病人のなかには、1日に12回入る人もいるのです！

　ここには湖があり、人々を乗せて遊覧する船があります。そのほかには、たいした娯楽はありません。人々は温泉に浸かったり、眠ったり、煙草を吸ったり、食べたりして過ごすしかないのです。

茶屋の女
Attendant at Tea-House

The *mago*, or man who manages the pack-horse, ties straw shoes onto the horse's feet and packs everything onto it. **This requires great skill** and balance. Riding the horse, too, takes great balance.

My journey ended at a beautiful *yadoya* that seems better suited for fairies than dirty, tired humans. The *fusuma* are made of sweet-smelling wood, and the balconies are polished pine. A smiling girl brought me plum-flower tea that tasted like almonds.

I spent the evening exploring the village and bathing houses. Yumoto is over 4,000 feet high in elevation and very cold. The village is full of people and the four bath-houses were crowded. Some unhealthy people bathe twelve times a day!

There is a lake here, and a boat that takes people sailing on it. Aside from that, there is not much amusement. People here must spend all their time bathing, sleeping, smoking, and eating.

日光、入町にて
6月23日

　日光での穏やかな日々も、もうすぐ終わりです。明日には、日本の奥地への旅に出るからです。ここの人たちは親切でしたから、村の生活についていろいろ学ぶことができました。

　入町村には、3本の道に沿って300軒ほどの家があります。それぞれの道の真ん中に小川が流れていて、子どもたちが水におもちゃを浮かべて遊んでいます。午前7時に太鼓が鳴ると、子どもたちは学校へ集まります。学校の建物はとても立派ですが、**西洋風の机と椅子は子どもたちにはすわり心地が悪そうです**。壁には上等な地図が掛かり、教師はとてもはつらつとしています。**服従が日本の社会秩序の基本なので**、子どもたちはみんな、きわめて従順です。子どもたちを静かにさせて注意を向けさせるのに、教師はなんの苦労もいりません。

　金谷邸で子どもたちの正式なパーティーが催され、興味津々で見せてもらいました。金谷氏の12歳の姪、ハルがお友だちを招いたのです。ハルは青い花柄で、袖が地面につきそうな着物を着ていました。顔と首はおしろいで白く塗り、唇に紅をさしています。招待客が全員やってくると、ハルと母親がお茶とお菓子をとても優雅に運んできました。それから、みんなで夕暮れまで静かに遊んでいまし

Irimichi, Nikko
June 23

My peaceful life in Nikko is almost over. I leave tomorrow to travel into the interior of Japan. The people here have been kind, and I've learned about village life.

The village of Irimichi has about three hundred houses built along three roads. A little stream runs down the middle of each road, and children float toys on the water. At 7 a.m., a drum calls all the children to school. The school building is very good, but the **children look uncomfortable sitting at European-style desks**. There are fine maps on the walls and the teacher is very bright. **Obedience is the base of Japanese social order**, and all the children are extremely obedient. The teacher has no problem getting the children to be quiet and attentive.

Kanaya's house hosts formal children's parties that are interesting to watch. Kanaya's twelve-year-old niece, Haru, invited her friends to a party. Haru wore a blue, flowered *kimono* with sleeves that touched the ground. Her face and neck were painted white and her lips were touched with red paint. When all the guests arrived, she and her mother served tea and sweets

た。ハルも年若いお客たちもみな、まるで人形のようでした。

ハルの母親のユキは魅力的で上品な人で、いつも家事をしています。日本の女の子はみな、裁縫を教わって自分の着物を縫います。**裁縫はイギリスのようにとんでもなく難しいものではありません**。着物はまっすぐ縫うだけですし、フリルも、ベルトも、ボタン穴もないからです。

ユキの息子は13歳くらいですが、よく習字の腕前を見せてくれます。筆に墨をつけると、2度か3度動かして、長さ1フィートくらいの文字を書くのです。ユキは三味線を弾き、ハルがその弾き方を習っているところです。

生け花は女の子が身につけるべき教養のひとつです。ほぼ毎日、わたしの部屋にも新しい花が生けられます。**さりげなく飾ることで生まれる極上の美しさ**が、わたしにも理解できるようになってきました。一本のアヤメや桜の枝が持つ自然な美しさに比べたら、イギリスの花束がけばけばしく感じられます。

朝、家族みんなが目を覚ますと、ふとんを押し入れにしまいます。それから床を掃いて、家具のほこりを払い、雨戸と窓を開けます。朝食を食べ、家事をします。昼食は1時に食べ、それから裁縫をしたり、庭の手入れをしたりして、6時になると夕食です。訪問客は夕食後にやってきます。たいていは将棋をしたり、三味線を弾いたり、歌ったり、話をしたりします。夜が更けると、米で作った酒を飲みます。これを温めて飲むと、あっという間に酔いがまわるのです！

very gracefully. Then they all played quiet games until dusk. Haru and all her young guests looked like dolls.

Yuki, Haru's mother, is charming and graceful. She is always doing housework. All Japanese girls learn how to sew and make their own clothes. **Sewing is not as dreadfully difficult as it is in England**, because the *kimono* only has straight seams and there are no frills, bands, or buttonholes.

Yuki's son, who is about thirteen, often shows me his skills in calligraphy. He dips his brush into ink, and with two or three moves creates characters that are a foot long. Yuki plays the *samisen*, and Haru is learning how to play.

The art of flower arrangement is a part of girls' education. A new arrangement appears in my room almost every day. I am starting to understand **the extreme beauty of simple decoration**. In comparison to the natural beauty of a single iris or cherry branch, the English bouquet seems very garish to me.

In the morning, the family wakes and puts their futon away in a closet. Then they sweep the floors, dust the furniture, and open the *amado* and windows. They eat breakfast, followed by housework. Lunch is eaten at one, then they sew or garden until dinner is eaten at six. Visitors arrive after dinner. They usually play Japanese chess, play *samisen*, sing, or tell stories. Towards the end of the evening, they drink *sake*, or rice wine. When served hot, *sake* goes straight to the head!

家のなかでただひとつ宗教らしいものは、「神棚」です。そこには小さな木製の神社が置かれ、亡くなった親族の位牌が納められています。

　日本の女の子はたいてい16歳で結婚します。これはしばらくあとで知ったのですが、かわいい女の子が**お歯黒をし、眉を落として、疲れたようすの女に変わってしまいます。**結婚してすぐにしなくても、ひとり目の子どもを産んだら、かならずそうするのです。

　これほど子どもを愛している人たちを見たことがありません！　日本人はつねに子どもを連れ歩き、手をつなぎ、遊びを見守ったり、一緒に遊んだりし、新しいおもちゃを与え、祭りに連れていきます。父親も母親も自分たちの子どもを誇りに思っています。わけあって男の子のほうが喜ばれますが、女の子もたいへん愛されています。子どもたちはとても従順で、よくお手伝いをし、お互いに親切で、本当に驚くほどです。でも、子どもというより、小さな大人のように見えます。親たちとまったく同じ服装をしていることで、なおさらそう感じるのでしょう。

The only sign of religion in the house is the *kamidana*, or "god shelf." It holds a little wooden Shinto shrine, in which there are tablets dedicated to dead relatives.

Japanese girls usually marry when they are sixteen. I discovered that soon afterwards, these pretty girls **turn into tired-looking women who blacken their teeth and remove their eyebrows**. If this is not done soon after marriage, it happens after the birth of the first child.

I never saw a people so loving to their children! The Japanese are always carrying them around, holding their hands, watching or joining their games, giving them new toys, and taking them to festivals. Both fathers and mothers are very proud of their children. For some reason they seem to prefer boys, but girls are also very well loved. The children are so obedient, so helpful, and so good to each other that it is quite astonishing. But they seem like little men and women rather than children. The fact that they dress exactly like their parents reinforces this.

藤原にて
6月24日

　快適さはすべて日光に置いてきてしまいました！　今朝、ひとりの女が、悲しそうな目をした雌馬を2頭連れてきたのです。伊藤とかばんをすべて1頭にのせ、もう1頭にわたしが乗り、日光の荘厳な神社を後にしました。道は険しくて岩が多く、大谷川を何度も仮設の橋で渡りました。谷を曲がりくねって進みましたが、その険しい斜面は、カエデ、ナラ、モクレン、ニレ、松、杉で覆われていました。藤の花が大きな房になって木からぶらさがっています。どこを見渡しても、雄大な山、滝、きれいな小川がありました。明るい6月の日差しのもとで、この国はなんて美しかったことでしょう。

　小百という山間の農村で馬を替えて、小佐越という小さな山村へ向かいました。ここの家々はとても貧しそうで、子どもたちは汚れ、皮膚病を患っていました。女たちの顔は**重労働と、薪の煙をたくさん浴びるせいで醜くなっていました。**

　男たちはほとんど服を着ておらず、女たちは腰のまわりに短い布【訳注：腰巻き】を巻いているだけでした。ときどき女たち

夏と冬の服装
Summer and Winter Costume

Fujihara
June 24

We left all comfort behind in Nikko! This morning a woman brought me two sad-looking mares. Ito and all my bags went onto one, I got on the other, and we left the glorious shrines of Nikko behind. Our path was rough and rocky, crossing the Daiyagawa many times on temporary bridges. We wound through valleys where the steep slopes are covered with maple, oak, magnolia, elm, pine, and cedar. Wisteria hangs from the trees in great clusters. Every view contained some grand mountain, waterfall, or clear stream. The country was beautiful in the bright June sunshine.

At the mountain farm of Kohiaku, we changed horses and traveled on to Kisagoi, a small mountain village. The houses here looked very poor, and the children were dirty or suffering from skin diseases. The women's faces were ugly **from severe work and too much wood smoke.**

The men wear almost no clothing, and the women just wear a short cloth around the waist. Sometimes, the women wear blue trousers that are tight around the legs and loose on top, and a short jacket open to the waist. You can't tell from these people's clothing

は、足のほうはきつくて上のほうがゆったりした青いズボン【訳注：もんぺ】をはき、腰のあたりまで開いた短い上着を着ていました。この人たちの服装や顔を見ても、男か女かわかりません。ただ、お歯黒や眉を剃っているのを見て、やっと女だとわかるくらいです。**自分が「文明化された」日本にいるとは、信じられないほどでした。**ほとんどの旅行者が見る光景とは、まったく違うのです。

鬼怒川（きぬ）を過ぎると、二荒山（ふたあらやま）という、神道の伝説の多い山が見えてきました。そしてついに、鬼怒川の上の棚田にある村に到着しました。11時間もかかって、18マイルしか進めなかったのです！

五十里（いかり）にて、6月25日——藤原には、46軒の農家と1軒の宿屋があります。どの家も暗くて汚く、じめじめしています。宿屋は蚤だらけで、すわることも眠ることもほとんどできませんでした。畳は茶色く、米も古くておいしくありません。

伊藤と一緒に、村やまわりの林を見てまわりました。村を流れる川が、村人の手洗いであり、水飲み場でもあります。畑仕事から戻ってくると、女たちが裸足で乾いた堆肥の山を崩します。幼い子どもたちは、**ひものついたお守り以外は何も身につけていません。**人も衣服も家も、みんな害虫だらけです。それに、うるさくて攻撃的な犬の群れがいます。

朝の5時に、伊藤がわたしの部屋へやってきて、もう出発したいと頼んできました。「まったく眠れませんでした。蚤が何千匹もいるんですよ！」彼はほかのルートで**日本奥地**を旅したことがありますが、こんなところは見たことがないそうです。この村や女たちの服装のことを横浜で話し

or faces whether they are male or female. I only know the women from their blackened teeth and shaved eyebrows. **I could hardly believe I was in "civilized" Japan**. This is totally different from what most tourists see.

We traveled past the Kinugawa and glimpsed Futarayama, a mountain in many Shinto legends. Finally, we arrived at a village located among rice terraces over the Kinugawa. After eleven hours, we had only traveled eighteen miles!

Ikari, June 25—Fujihara has forty-six farmhouses and one *yadoya*. All are dark, dirty, and damp. The fleas at the *yadoya* made it very hard to sit or sleep. The mats were brown, and the rice tasted old.

I explored the village and surrounding woods with Ito. A stream that runs through the village serves as both public bath and drinking water. After the people come back from farming, the women break up piles of dried manure with their bare feet. The young children **wear nothing but a string and an amulet**. All the people, clothing, and houses are hosts to insects, and there are packs of loud, aggressive dogs.

At five this morning, Ito came to my room and begged to leave. "I haven't slept. There are thousands of fleas!" he said. He traveled into **the interior of Japan** on a different route, and he says he never saw a place like this. He says the people of Yokohoma

ても、信じてもらえないだろうと言います。そして、「外国の人にこんなところを見られるのは恥です」と言うのです。

　伊藤はたいへん賢くて、いい英語を話そうと心に決めています。毎日わからない単語を紙に書いて、夜に勉強しているのです。もう今では、多くのプロの通訳よりずっと上手に英語を話します。彼はとても愛国主義者で、外国のものは何でも劣っていると思っています。イギリス人の行儀の悪さについて話すのが大好きで、彼らがどんなに騒がしくて、乱暴で、無礼で、日本の作法を知らないかを語るのです。わたしも不作法に見えないかと心配なので、伊藤の忠告はすべて聞くようにしています。きっと、**わたしのお辞儀は日々に低く、深くなっていることでしょう**！

　今日は鬼怒川沿いに進んで、五十里村へ向かいました。川はつねに澄んだ青色か、緑色です。日本で一番すばらしいもののひとつだといえるでしょう。

　五十里は山のなかにある美しい村です。今夜は、山の上の駅逓所(えきていじょ)で休みます。これは大きな納屋で、片方に厩(うまや)があり、反対側が居間になっています。地方の大名が旅行中に宿泊したそうで、部屋はきちんとして清潔ですし、障子もふすまも上質なものです。伊藤は町の人たちに、わたしのことを学者だと、誇らしげに言っていました！

won't believe it when he tells them of it, and how the women are dressed. He says he is "ashamed for a foreigner to see such a place."

Ito is extremely clever and determined to speak good English. Every day he writes words that he doesn't understand, then studies them at night. He already speaks English much better than many professional interpreters. He is very patriotic and thinks anything foreign is inferior. He loves to tell stories of the bad manners of Englishmen, telling of how they are loud, violent, disrespectful, and ignorant of Japanese etiquette. I'm also nervous about seeming impolite, so I listen to all his advice. I believe **my bows are growing lower and deeper every day**!

Today we traveled along the Kinugawa to the village of Ikari. The river is always crystal-blue or crystal-green. I believe it is one of the loveliest things in Japan.

Ikari is beautifully located in the mountains. Tonight, I am resting at the Transport Office at the top of the hill. It's a large barn with horses at one end and living rooms at the other. A local *daimyo* used to stay here when he was traveling, so the rooms are neat and clean, with fine *shoji* and *fusuma*. Ito has proudly announced to the townspeople that I am a *gakusha*—a scholar!

3章
車峠から市野々へ
(福島県)　　　(新潟県)

From Kurumatoge to Ichinono

車峠にて
6月30日

　もう6日間も、苦しい旅をしています。頭のなかは、山や、谷、田んぼ、貧しさ、重労働する農民、汚さ、古い寺、荷馬、そしてわたしを見つめる人の群れなどで雑然としています。幸運なことに、五十里から横川へ向かうあいだは好天に恵まれました。横川に着き、茶屋の外で昼食を食べていると、村人たちがわたしを見に集まってきました。そのあとで、山道を2,500フィート登りました。もうここでは、大きな川も小川も、太平洋ではなく日本海に注いでいるはずです。糸沢で馬がとてもよろめきだしたので、とうとう馬から降り、川島までの残りの道を歩くことになりました。川島はみすぼらしい村でしたが、あまりに疲れていたので、もう進むことができず、その夜はここに泊まりました。

　宿屋はひどいものでした。台所から流れてくる煙がもうもうと立ちこめていて、部屋もとても汚れていました。宿の主人が、家の汚さを詫びました。米も大豆もありません。そのありさまに伊藤が腹をたて、主人や使用人たちに無礼な態度を取りはじめました。わたしはすぐに、それをやめさせました。使用人が無礼にふるまうことほど、外国人にとって胸の痛むことはありません——また人々にとっても、これほど不親切なことはないでしょう。それでなく

Kurumatoge
June 30

I have been traveling hard for six days. My mind now is a jumble of mountains, valleys, rice fields, poverty, hardworking farmers, dirt, old temples, pack-horses, and crowds of people staring at me. I was lucky to have nice weather as I traveled from Ikari to Yokokawa. In Yokokawa, I ate lunch outside the tea-house and a crowd of villagers came to stare at me. Afterwards, we climbed 2,500 feet over a mountain pass. I believe the rivers and streams now run into the Sea of Japan, rather than the Pacific Ocean. At Itosawa, our horses **stumbled so much** that I ended up getting off and walking the rest of the way to Kayashima. It was a miserable village, but I was so tired that I couldn't go on. We stayed the night there.

Our *yadoya* was awful. It was filled with smoke from the *daidokoro* and my room was very dirty. The owner apologized for the dirtiness of his house. There was no rice or soy. These conditions upset Ito, and he began behaving rudely to the house-master and servants. I made him stop this right away. **There is nothing so damaging to** a foreigner—or so unkind to the people—as a servant who acts rudely. Despite

ても、宿の主人は礼儀正しくて、わたしに近づくときはいつも膝をついているのですから。

　主人の息子がひどい咳をしていたので、クロロダイン【訳注：麻酔鎮痛薬】を数滴飲ませました。それでとてもよくなったので、この話が村じゅうに広がりました。翌朝になると、村人が全員わたしの部屋の外に集まり、咳や、皮膚病、盲目、白癬(はくせん)、痛みなどで具合の悪い子どもたちを連れてきたのです。病気であろうとなかろうと、みんな汚れています。残念ながら、病気の治し方はわからないと伝えました。ただ自分の国では、つねに衣服を洗い、体もこすり洗いして病気を防いでいると話しました。

this, the house-master remained polite and always approached me on his knees.

The house-master's son had a bad cough, so I gave him a few drops of chlorodyne. This cured him so well that the news spread through the entire village. The next morning all the villagers were gathered outside my room. They brought children who were ill with coughs, skin diseases, blindness, ringworm, and sores. Everyone, whether sick or not, was dirty. Sadly, I told them I didn't know how to cure their illnesses. But I told them that in my country, constant washing of clothes and scrubbing of the body prevents many diseases.

車峠にて
6月30日

　旅の次の行程はとても美しいものでしたが、道も馬もよくないので道中はたいへんでした。いい馬なら1時間で平野を横切れるのに、わたしたちの馬は7時間もかかったのです。

　高田(たかた)という、絹と綱を商う大きな町で、足を止めて休みました。ここには、県の高官のひとりが住んでいるそうです。通りは1マイルの長さがあり、どの家も店になっています。町に入ると、最初に出会った男の人が、「外国人がいるぞ！」と日本語で叫びながら、通りを走っていきました。宿屋に着くころには、大勢の人混みがわたしのまわりに集まっていました。**プライバシーを守れるように**、宿屋の主人が庭にある美しい離れの部屋へ連れていってくれました。それでも、大人たちは近くの屋根に上ってこちらを見おろし、子どもたちは塀によじ登って、塀を壊してしまうありさまです。

　わたしがもう一度外に出るころには、なんと千人もの人が集まっていました！　でも、日本人の群れは静かでおとなしいのです。いつもわたしが動けるだけの距離を置きますし、けっして失礼なことはしません。

　このあとさらに5時間、稲田の道を進みました。そして坂下(ばんげ)という、人口約5,000人の町に着きました。水田のなかにある町で、泥の臭いがします。ここではマラリアが流

Kurumatoge
June 30

The next part of my journey was very pretty, but bad roads and bad horses made the trip difficult. While one good horse could have crossed the plain in one hour, it took our horses seven hours.

We stopped to rest at Takata, a large trading town dealing in silk and rope. One of the higher prefecture officials lives here. The street is a mile long, and every house is a shop. As I entered town, the first man who saw me ran down the street, yelling "Here's a foreigner!" in Japanese. By the time I reached the *yadoya*, a large crowd had gathered around me. **For some privacy,** the house-master led me to a pretty room in a garden. But then the adults climbed on the nearby roofs to look down at me, and the children climbed a fence, which broke.

By the time I went outside again, a thousand people had gathered! But the Japanese crowds are quiet and gentle. They always give me enough space to move and are never rude.

After this, we traveled for another five hours through rice fields. We reached Bange, a town of about 5,000 people. It is located in a rice swamp and smells

行っているのです――あまりにひどいので、政府が特別に医療援助をしたほどです。その夜は込んだ宿屋に泊りましたが、息苦しいくらい蚊がたくさんいました。夜が明けるなり、早く出発したくてしかたがありませんでした。

出発する用意をしていると、町の半分ほどの人たちが出てきて、じっと見つめていました。わたしが望遠鏡をケースから取り出すと、みんな怖がって逃げていきました。ピストルを取り出そうとしたと思ったのだと、伊藤が説明してくれました。そこで伊藤に、望遠鏡とはなんのかを説明してもらいました。町の人たちを怖がらせたくなかったからです。日本人は本当に穏やかな人たちです。ヨーロッパの多くの国では、独身の女がひとりで旅行するのは危険なものです。でもここでは、なんの問題も起きたことがないのです。

再びひどい道を一日じゅう旅して、やっと野尻という美しい村に到着しました。**何にもまして、日本にはよい道路が必要です。**でもその道中で、会津山の雄大な眺めを楽しむことができました。

野尻に入ると、険しい崖の縁にある、きれいな茶屋を見つけました。ここからの眺めは最高です。このような美しいところに、**厳しい貧しさがあるとは信じがたいことです。**でも、縄のぶらさがる木のそばを通りすぎたとき、その証拠を目にしました。つい先日、ある男がそこで首を吊ったというのです。貧しすぎて大家族を支えられず、自殺したのです。伊藤の話では、そういう人たちが自殺するのはよくあることだそうです。

茶屋の主人は、朗らかな女の人です。中国やロシアのことは知っているけれど、イギリスのことは聞いたことがないそうです。

like mud. There is malaria here—it is so bad that the government has sent special medical help. I stayed the night in a crowded *yadoya* where the air was thick with mosquitos. I was eager to leave the next morning.

As we made preparations to leave, about half the town came out to stare. When I took out my telescope from my case, everyone ran away in fear. Ito explained that they thought I was pulling out a gun. I made him explain what the telescope was, because I didn't want to scare them. The Japanese are truly a gentle people. In many European countries, it's dangerous for a single woman to travel alone. But here, I haven't had any trouble.

We traveled again over horrible roads all day until we reached a pretty village called Nojiri. **More than anything**, Japan needs good roads. But along the way we had magnificent views of the Aidzu Mountains.

In Nojiri, we found a lovely tea-house that sits on the edge of a steep cliff. The views here are incredible. **It is hard to believe that severe poverty could exist** in such a pretty place. But we saw evidence of this when we passed a tree with a rope hanging from it. A man had recently hung himself there. He was too poor to support his large family, so he killed himself. Ito tells me that suicide is common among such men.

The tea-house master is a cheerful woman. Although she knows of China and Russia, she says she has never heard of England.

津川にて
7月2日

　車峠から西へ進む道も、やはり最悪でした。車峠は、わたしたちが越えてきた高度2000フィート以上ある17の山道のなかで、最後のものです。車峠から津川までの景色は、日本のほかの地域と同じように、**植物がびっしり生えています**。何か目新しいものや違ったもの——砂漠や、切り立った崖など——が現れて、緑ばかりのこの単調さを破ってくれないものかと、何度も思います。

　このあたりで見た町や人々ほど、**未開のものは見たことがありません**。大人たちは虫にかまれた跡だらけで、子どもたちは皮膚病に冒されています。誰もが不潔なのです。馬、犬、人がみんな一緒に煙たい小屋に住んでいます。この人たちの精神状態は、身体の状態よりもいいのだろうかと、思わずにはいられません。

　今夜の宿屋の主人は武士で、身分の低い人たちとは違う**話し方をします**。その奥さんが、わたしのことを外国人にしてはとても礼儀正しいと言ってくれます。理由を訊くと、家のなかに入るまえに靴を脱ぐし、煙草盆を渡すとお辞儀をするからだそうです。

　これで陸の旅のうち、最初の部分を終えました。明日は船で新潟へ向かいます。

Tsugawa
July 2

The road leading west from Kurumatoge was the worst road yet. Kurumatoge was the last of seventeen mountains passes we crossed over 2,000 feet high. The landscape from Kurumatoge to Tsugawa is **thick with vegetation,** like everywhere else in Japan. I often wish that something new and different—a desert, or a sudden cliff—would break this monotony of green.

The towns and people I saw on this part of the journey were **the least civilized I've seen**. Adults were covered in bug bites, and children were covered in skin diseases. Everyone was dirty. Horses, dogs, and people all gathered together in smoky sheds. I couldn't help but wonder if these peoples' spiritual condition was any better than their physical condition.

The house-master of my *yadoya* tonight is a samurai. He has **a different way of speaking than** the lower classes. His wife says I am very polite for a foreigner. I asked why, and she said it was because I took off my shoes before coming inside, and because I bowed when they passed me the *tabako-bon*.

I have finished the first part of my land journey. I leave for Niigata by boat tomorrow.

新潟にて
7月4日

　船に間に合うよう、今朝は早く出発しました。今日はすばらしい天気で、日差しが明るく、不快な暑さもありません。

　船はしっかりした造りで、長さ45フィート、幅6フィートの大きさです。ふたりの男が立ったまま船を操っています。船の前部には、米俵や、陶器を入れた箱が積まれていました。そして後部に**屋根のついた場所**があり、25人の日本人の乗客がすわっています。そのほとんどが川辺の村落で降りました。わたしは積み荷の上に椅子を置いてすわり、山と田んぼばかりで飽き飽きしていたのが、この船旅で変化したことを喜んでいました。

　船は**見るからに純和風**で、日焼けした船頭たちがいて、わらぶきの屋根があり、乗客の雨笠がたくさん帆柱にぶらさがっています。船に乗っているあいだ、ずっと楽しい気分でした。静かに流れを下っていくのは、とても気持ちのいいものです。清々しい空気もおいしくて、津川は想像していたよりずっとすてきな川でした。

　あるところで、すばらしい山に行く手を遮られたと思いましたが、ちょうど通れるくらいのすき間がありました。まわりには**岩だらけの山頂、生い茂る植物**、深い峡谷、仏塔、日の当たる村々があり、雪をかぶった山脈がはるか

Niigata
July 4

We left early this morning to catch our boat. Today is a gorgeous day, bright with sunshine without the uncomfortable heat.

Our boat is well-built, measuring 45 feet long by 6 feet wide. Two men steer the boat standing up. The front of the boat was loaded with bags of rice and boxes of pottery. The back had **a roofed portion** where twenty-five Japanese passengers sat. Most of them got off at hamlets on the river. I put my chair on top of the cargo, and I found the voyage to be a delightful change from the tiring journey through mountains and rice fields.

The boat **looks very Japanese**, with a brown-skinned crew, a thatched roof, and the passengers' umbrella hats all hanging on the mast. I enjoyed every hour. It was wonderful to float quietly downstream. The fresh air was delicious and the Tsugawa River was lovelier than I imagined.

At one point, I thought our way was blocked by some fantastic mountains, but there was an opening through them just wide enough to let us through. All around were **craggy peaks, lush vegetation**, deep

遠くに見えました。その景色は、クィラング【訳注：スコットランドのスカイ島にある山】やライン川より美しいものでした。

　川辺の暮らしもとても魅力的です。たくさんの丸木船が浮いていて、野菜を積んでいる舟や、小麦を積んでいる舟、ほかには学校帰りの少年少女を乗せている舟もあります。**白い帆をかけた平底船の船団が通りすぎていきます。**暑くて静かな午後、船頭とわたし以外に目を覚ましている人は誰もいません。夢見るような気持ちよさでした。

　多くの運河のひとつを通って、新潟に入りました。西日本のこの大きな町は、まわりの田園地方ほど美しくはありません。でも、教会宣教館のファイソン夫妻が温かく迎えてくれました。小さな家ですが、こうしてまたドアと壁があるというのは、なんてうれしいことでしょう！

ravines, pagodas, sunny villages, and glimpses of far-away snowy mountains. It was more beautiful than Quiraing or the Rhine.

River life is very pretty too. There were plenty of canoes, some loaded with vegetables, some with wheat, others with boys and girls returning from school. **Flotillas of sampans with white sails floated by.** Except the boatmen and myself, no one was awake during the hot, silent afternoon. It was dreamy and delicious.

We entered Niigata by one of its many canals. This great city of western Japan is not as beautiful as the surrounding countryside. But I was kindly welcomed by Mr. and Mrs. Fyson at the Church Mission House. The house is small, but it's nice to have doors and walls again!

新潟にて
7月9日

　明日、新潟を出発します。蚊がいるのには閉口しますが、新潟は洗練された町です。**条約港なのに、外国との貿易はありません**。外国の商社はふたつあるだけで、どちらもドイツのものですし、外国人は18人しかいません。ここの主な川である信濃川は、日本最長の川です。とても荒々しい川で、とてつもない量の水と砂利を運びます。技術者たちは、この川を制御して、川床を深くする方法を見つけようとしています。政府がここに港を造りたいと考えているからです。でも、それは難しいでしょうし、費用もずいぶんかかることでしょう。

　ここの学校はとてもよく整っていて、近代的な実験室を持つ工学校や、地質資料館があります。ヨーロッパ人医師が経営する立派な病院や、裁判所、大きな銀行、そして軍の兵舎がいくつかあります。とはいえ、政府が整えた新潟の町は、**伝統的で日本的な新潟に比べたら魅力がありません**。政府の建物には西洋の影響が感じられますが、町の伝統的な地域のほうは、これまで見たことがないほどすっきりとして、清潔で、居心地のよさそうなところなのです。美しい茶屋でも有名です。通りでは荷馬を見かけたことがありません。**何もかも舟で運ぶからです**。道の真ん中を流れる運河は、一日じゅう混雑しています。

Niigata
July 9

I leave Niigata tomorrow. Although the mosquitos are bad, Niigata is a handsome city. **It's a Treaty Port but has no foreign trade**. There are only two foreign firms here, both German, and only eighteen foreigners. The main river, the Shinano, is the largest in Japan. It is a very wild river that carries an enormous amount of water and gravel. Engineers are trying to figure a way of controlling the river and deepening the channel because the government would like to build a harbor here. But that would be challenging and costly.

The schools here are very good, including an engineering school with modern laboratories and a geological museum. There's a fine hospital run by a European doctor, a courthouse, a large bank, and some army barracks. But governmental Niigata **is unattractive compared to traditional, Japanese Niigata**. The government buildings show signs of Western influence, while the traditional part of town is the neatest, cleanest, most comfortable looking place I've seen yet. It's renowned for its beautiful tea-houses. I haven't seen any pack-horses in the streets because **everything comes in by boat**. The canals, running in

どの家にも小さな庭があり、ささやかな敷地にうまく配置されています。日本の庭にはたいてい、池、橋、石灯籠、ねじ曲がった松の木があり、裕福な家では、日陰ですわれるように小さな東屋(あずまや)を作っているところもあります。池には金や銀の魚が泳いでいたり、小さな島まであったりするのです。

ファイソン夫人と彼女の3才の娘ルースと一緒に、新潟の町をよく散歩しました。すると日本人たちが喜んでルースについてきて、その金髪を眺めるのです。ルースは彼らにとてもなついていて、お辞儀したり、日本語を話したりします。日本人は本当に子ども好きなのです！

街路と運河
Street and Canal

the middle of the roads, are busy all day.

Each house has a little garden, which is skillfully laid out in tiny spaces. Most Japanese gardens have a pond, a bridge, a stone lantern, and a crooked pine tree. Some wealthier houses have small pavilions for sitting in the shade. Some ponds have silver and gold fish, and even little islands.

I often walk about Niigata with Mrs. Fyson and her three-year-old daughter, Ruth. The Japanese love to follow Ruth and look at her golden hair. Ruth feels very much at home with them, and even bows and speaks Japanese. The Japanese love children!

市野々にて
7月12日

　ファイソン夫妻に別れの挨拶をして、平底船に乗りました。信濃川を横切り、新川をさかのぼっていきます。とても寂しい気持ちでした。6時間後、木崎に着き、ここから人力車で築地に向かいました。その途中、医療伝道から帰ってきたパーム医師に出会いました。これから数週間、彼以外のヨーロッパ人に会うことはないでしょう。

　黒川で宿屋に泊りましたが、**そこには米がないので、キュウリを食べました**。この地域ほどたくさんのきゅうりを食べるところは見たことがありません！　子どもたちは一日じゅうかじっていますし、母親におんぶされた赤ん坊でさえ熱心にしゃぶっているのです。

　わたしたちは今、900マイル以上にわたる日本の大山脈のなかにいます。これを越えるには、海抜1,000フィートから5,000フィートの山道を登っていくしかありません。これまで見たことがないほどに、悪路で遮断されたへんぴな地域なのです。

　沼という村落へ歩いて入っていきましたが、そこの人たちは外国人を見たことがありませんでした。わたしが話すのを聞きたがるので、みんなの前で伊藤に指示を出しました。**どこへ行くにも人々がついてくるのに、だんだん慣れてきました**。宿屋で自分の部屋にいるときでさえ、ふすま

Ichinono
July 12

I said goodbye to the Fysons this morning and boarded a sampan. As we crossed the Shinano River and went up the Shinkawa, I felt lonely. After six hours, we reached Kisaki. From here, we traveled by *kuruma* to Tsuiji. On the way, we met Dr. Palm returning from one of his medical expeditions. He will be the last European I see for some weeks.

I stayed at a *yadoya* in Kurokawa, and **since there was no rice, I ate cucumbers**. I never saw so many cucumbers eaten than in that district! Children chew on them all day long, and even babies on their mother's backs suck them hungrily.

We are now in the middle of Japan's great central chain of mountains that stretch over 900 miles. The only way to cross them is to climb over mountain passes that are 1,000 to 5,000 feet high. I've never seen a more remote region cut off by bad roads.

We walked into the hamlet of Numa, where the people had never seen a foreigner. They wanted to hear me speak, so I gave my orders to Ito in public. **I am starting to get used to crowds of people following me wherever I go**. Even when I am in my room at a

や障子の穴から多くの目がこちらを見つめているのです。

　沼で、おもしろいことを学びました。わたしは、日本の平均的な家庭は5人家族だと思っていました。ところが、日本のどの家の外にもぶらさがっている**表札を、伊藤に訳してもらうと、24軒の家に307人住んでいることがわかったのです！**　伊藤が言うには、祖父母、両親、子どもたち、そして義理の家族も同じ家に住むことが多いそうです。男が結婚すると、女はたいてい夫の両親の家へ行って暮らします。そして、**義理の母にとってまるで奴隷のような存在になるのです。**

　ここには荷馬がほとんどいないので、男も女も重い荷物を自分で運びます。この貧しい人たちが大きな荷物を抱えて山道を越えていく光景は、悲惨なものです。疲労で倒れそうなのに、それでも進み続けるのです。この不思議な国の人々は本当に働き者で、人に頼りません。日本では、物乞いを見たことがないのです。

　沼では馬が手に入らなかったので、かわいい雌牛があてがわれました。雌牛はわたしを乗せて、壮大な大里の山道を無事に運んでくれました。小国の町からは、雌牛に乗ったり歩いたりして市野々へ向かいました。

yadoya, I see many eyes watching me through holes in the *fusuma* and *shoji*.

In Numa, I learned something interesting. I thought the average Japanese household contained about five people. But **I had Ito translate the household roster** that is hung outside every Japanese house. We discovered that there were 307 people living in 24 houses! Ito tells me that grandparents, parents, children, and in-laws often live together in the same house. When a man marries, the woman usually goes to live in her husband's parents' house. There, **she becomes something very much like a slave to her mother-in-law**.

There are very few pack-horses here, so men and women carry heavy loads. It is terrible to see these poor people carrying enormous loads over the mountain passes. They look like they could fall over from exhaustion, yet they go on. The people of this strange country are truly hardworking and independent. I've never seen a beggar in Japan.

I could not get a horse in Numa, so I was given a pretty cow. It carried me safely over the magnificent Ori pass. From the town of Okimi, I traveled by cow and on foot to Ichinono.

4章
上山から
(山形県)
神宮寺、黒石へ
(秋田・青森県)

From Kaminoyama to Shingoji, Kuroishi

上山(かみのやま)にて

　すばらしい朝、荷物を運ぶ3頭のかわいい雌牛とともに、市野々を出発しました。新鮮なミルクがほしかったのですが、**雌牛の乳をしぼるということなど、ここの人たちは考えたこともないので**、みんなに笑われてしまいました。伊藤が、彼らは乳をしぼるなんて気持ち悪いと思っているのだ、と言います。日本人は、外国人が「あんなに臭くて味の強いもの」をお茶に入れるなんて、「とんでもなく気持ち悪い」と思っているそうなのです！

　手ノ子(てのこ)村で、駅逓所にすわって馬を待ちました。伊藤がぞっとするようなものを食べているあいだ、わたしは酒、お茶、ごはん、黒豆を食べました。黒豆はとても美味しかったです。そこにいる男の人が、彼の名前を英語で書いてほしい、また、わたしの名前を帳面に書いてほしいと言いました。**このせいで、人が集まりだしました**。その家の女の人たちは、わたしが暑そうにしているのを見て、まる1時間もあおいでくれました。それへのお礼をしようとしましたが、お金を受けとろうとしません。それだけでなく、お菓子の包みをくれたのです。男の人は自分の名前を扇子に書いて、わたしにプレゼントしてくれました。わたしがあげられるものは、イギリスのヘアピンだけです。もっといいものを贈れたらよかったのにと思いましたが、それでも彼らはそんなものを見たことがないと言って、たちまち

Kaminoyama

We left Ichinono on a fine morning, with three pretty pack-cows. I wanted some fresh milk, but **the idea of milking a cow was so new to the people** that they all laughed. Ito told me they thought it disgusting. The Japanese, he told me, think it "most disgusting" that foreigners put anything "with such a strong smell and taste" into their tea!

At the village of Tenoko, I sat at the Transport Office waiting for a horse. While Ito ate dishes of horrible things, I had some *sake*, tea, rice, and black beans. The beans were very good. The man there asked me to write his name in English, and to write my own in a book. **This drew a crowd**. When the women of the house saw that I was hot, they fanned me for a whole hour. I tried to pay them for their services, but they wouldn't take any money. Not only that, but they gave me a package of sweets. The man wrote his name on a fan and gave it to me as a gift. All I could give them was some English pins. I wished I could give them something more, but they had never seen such things, and they soon passed them around the crowd.

人々のあいだに回しはじめました。わたしは、あなたたちのことはいつまでも忘れませんと言って、この人たちのやさしさに胸を打たれながら、出発したのです。

越後（えちご）地方のあちらこちらで、一枚の布の4隅を4本の竹の棒でつるし、小川の上に広げたものを目にしました。布には文字が書かれていることもあります。たいていはその後ろに、文字の書かれた細長い板が立てられ、花束のあることもあります。そして必ず木製のひしゃくが置いてあります。手ノ子から来る途中でそういう布のそばを通ったとき、**僧侶がひしゃくに入れた水を布にかけているのを見ました**。水はゆっくりと布を通して落ちていきます。わたしたちは、これはなんですかと僧侶に訊きました。

僧侶の話によれば、板には戒名——人の死後の名前——が書かれているそうです。布の文字は日蓮宗のお題目、南無妙法蓮華経です。布に水をかけて祈ることを、「流れ灌頂（かんじょう）」といいます。これは、初めて妊娠したのに出産で亡くなってしまった母親のための供養なのです。そういう女は、仏教の地獄のひとつである血の池地獄で、前世の罪を罰せられて苦しむと信じられています。そして布がすり切れて水がすぐに通るようになるまで、地獄にとどまるそうです。そばを通る者は誰でも、その女

流し祈願
The Flowing Invocation

I told them that I will remember them forever, and I left, touched by their kindness.

Throughout Echigo province, I have seen a piece of cloth suspended over a stream by four bamboo poles. Sometimes the cloth has characters on it. A long, narrow tablet with writing usually stands behind it, and sometimes there are bouquets of flowers. There is always a wooden dipper. I passed one of these coming from Tenoko, and I watched **a Buddhist priest pour a dipper full of water onto** it. The water strained slowly through the cloth. We asked him to explain what it was.

According to him, the tablet has a *kaimiyo* on it—the name of a person after death. The characters on the cloth are the Nichiren prayer, *Namu mio ho ren ge kio*. Pouring water onto the cloth and praying is called "The Flowing Invocation." It is a prayer for a first-time mother who has died in childbirth. It is believed that the woman suffers in the Lake of Blood, one of the Buddhist hells, where she is being punished for a sin in an earlier life. She will remain in hell until the cloth is so worn out that the water falls straight through it. Anybody passing by can offer her a prayer. It is one of the saddest, most moving things I have ever seen.

のために祈りを捧げることができます。これまで見たなかで、もっとも悲しくて、心を動かされることのひとつでした。

米沢平野を見おろしたとき、まるでエデンの園を見ているような気がしました。この地方では、米、綿、とうもろこし、煙草、麻、藍、豆、なすび、ほかにもいろいろなものが豊かに産出されるのです。ここには美と、生産性と、居心地のよさがあります。村々は美しいうえに、大きくて住みやすそうな家がたくさん建っています。

今夜は赤湯という温泉町に泊まる予定です。このようなところを見るのは、とてもおもしろいものです。ここには**独特な伝統的習慣や、楽しみ、文化**があって、西洋の影響はまったく受けていないのです。とはいえ、今まで見たなかで一番騒々しいところでもあります。

上山の美しい娘
The Belle of Kaminoyama

When we looked down upon the plain of Yonezawa, I felt like I was looking at the Garden of Eden. The region is rich in rice, cotton, corn, tobacco, hemp, indigo, beans, eggplants, and more. There is beauty, industry, and comfort here. The villages are beautiful, with large, comfortable homes.

I am staying tonight at Akayu, a hot spring town. It is very interesting to see places like this, which have **their own traditional habits, amusements, and civilization**—all without any Western influence. But it is one of the noisiest places I've ever been.

金山にて
7月16日

　すばらしい道を3日間旅したので、60マイルも進むことができました。山形県はじつに裕福で進歩的なようです。道がいいのは、ここでは囚人たちが道路整備のために働いているからです。囚人たちは漢字の入った赤い着物を着て、地元の農家や建築業者のためにも働いています。

　山形の北部には平野がさらに広がっています。多くの農村があり、鳥海山——雪をかぶった雄大な山——のすばらしい景色が見られます。ここの建物は独特で、もう木造ではなく、泥と、切り藁で造られています。木の枠で支えて、とてもきれいにできています。また、この農家には障子の窓はなく、雨戸だけがあるのです。

　新庄というみすぼらしい町に泊まりました。大名が住んだ城下町ですが、**城下町はみな衰退の一途をたどっているようです。城が取り壊されたり、朽ちるままに放って置かれるのが原因のひとつでしょう。**

　今夜は金山に泊まります。この地は美しく、駅遞所でのわたしの部屋は気持ちいいですし、そのうえ伊藤が、日光を出発してから初めて鶏を手に入れてくれたのです！

　わたしの病弱な体では、こんなにじめじめした気候のな

Kanayama
July 16

After three days of traveling on excellent roads, I covered sixty miles. Yamagata-ken seems quite wealthy and progressive. The roads are good, and the prisoners here work on improving them. They wear red *kimonos* with Chinese characters and work for local farmers and builders.

North of Yamagata, the plain widens. There are many farming villages and incredible views of Chokaizan—a grand, snow-covered mountain. The buildings here are unique. They are no longer made of wood, but of mud with chopped straw. They are held up by wooden frames and are very neat. These farmhouses have no paper windows, only *amado*.

I stayed in Shinjo, a wretched place. It is a *daimyo*'s town, and **all *daimyo*'s towns look like they are dying.** This is partly because **the castle is either being pulled down or being left to rot**.

Tonight I'm staying in Kanayama. The location is beautiful, my rooms at the Transport Office are cheerful, and Ito got us a chicken for the first time since we left Nikko!

With my poor health, it is impossible to travel for

かで、2、3日以上続けて旅はできません。どこへ行っても蚤と蚊がいます。また、スズメバチや「ウマアリ」もいて、刺されると痛い腫物(はれもの)ができます。左手を2回刺されてしまい、ひどく腫れているのです。

more than two or three days in a row in this damp weather. Everywhere we go, there are fleas and mosquitos. There are also hornets and "horse ants," whose bites create painful sores. I've been stung twice on my left hand, and it is very inflamed.

神宮寺にて
7月21日

　伊藤が朝早くわたしを起こして、こう言いました。「今日は遠くまで行けるでしょう。昨日鶏肉を召し上がったんですから」。わたしたちは午前6時45分に出発しましたが、道が悪く、山道をふたつも越えなければならなかったので、15マイルしか進めませんでした。

　院内の宿屋はとても気持ちのいいものでした。隣の部屋には6人の技術者がいました。彼らは山のあたりを調査して、トンネルを掘れるかどうか見ているのです。トンネルができれば、東京から日本海側の久保田まで、人力車で行けるようになるでしょう。

　六郷で、幸運なことに仏式の葬儀に出ることができました。六郷の警察が手配してくれたのです。わたしは着物と青い頭巾をかぶっていたので、目立つことはなかったでしょう。**着物はとても窮屈でしたが、**伊藤がくれた作法についての指示をしっかり守りました。

　亡くなった人は商人でした。人が死ぬと、遺体の頭を北に向けて寝かせます。(生きているあいだ、日本人は北向きに寝るのを避けるのです)。線香をあげ、米粉を練った生の団子のお供えをそばに置きます。僧侶が戒名という死後の名前を選び、遺体のそばにすわります。48時間後、遺体をぬるま湯で洗います。そのあと、僧侶はお経を唱えながら、遺体の頭を剃ります。裕福でも貧しくても、死人は

Shingoji
July 21

Ito woke me early in the morning, saying, "You'll be able to travel far today, because you had chicken yesterday." We set off at 6:45 a.m., but because the roads were bad and we had two mountain-passes to cross, we only went fifteen miles.

My *yadoya* at Innai was very cheerful. There were six engineers staying in the next room. They are surveying the nearby mountain to see if it could be tunneled. That could allow a *kuruma* to go from Tokiyo to Kubota on the Sea of Japan.

At Rokugo, I was lucky enough to attend a Buddhist funeral. The police of Rokugo arranged it for me, and I wore a *kimono* and a blue hood so I would blend in. **I found the *kimono* very restricting**, but I closely followed all of Ito's instructions of etiquette.

The man who had died was a merchant. When a person dies, the body is laid so the head points north. (While living, the Japanese avoid lying down this way.) Offerings of incense and rice dough are placed nearby. Buddhist monks choose the *kaimiyo*, or death name, and sit beside the corpse. After forty-eight hours, the corpse is washed with warm water. Then

みんな白装束を着せられます。

　その人の棺は、四角い木の箱でした。貧しい人は「早桶」というもの——竹の輪をはめた松材の桶——を使うそうです。遺体は箱や桶のなかに**正座の姿勢**で納められます。

　小さな旗と装飾品が家の玄関に飾ってありました。ふたりの男の人が水の入った漆の器と、白い絹の布を差し出します。この人たちは青い着物の上に、翼のような羽織を着ています。それから、豪華な絵の屏風を何枚も置いた部屋へ入りました。棺は、部屋の奥にある白い天蓋の下に安置されていました。壮麗な衣装を着た6人の僧侶が棺の両側にすわっています。さらに2人の僧侶が、小さな祭壇の前でひざまずいていました。

　未亡人が棺のそばにすわっていました。空色の着物に上質な白い羽織を着て、たいへん美しい人です。家族や友人のほとんどが青か白の着物を着ているので、**部屋の雰囲気は悲しくて陰鬱というより、色鮮やかでお祭りのようでした**。お茶とお菓子が配られ、お経が唱えられ、香が焚かれました。それから、墓地への葬列が始まりました。

　戒名の書かれた位牌を持った僧侶が、行列の先頭に立ちました。その次は、蓮の花を持った僧侶です。10人の僧侶がそれに続き、経本を手にお経を唱えながら、ふたりずつ並んで歩いていきます。そのあとから、台に載せた棺が

the priest shaves the head of the corpse while saying prayers. Whether rich or poor, all the dead are dressed in a white garment.

The man's coffin was a square box of wood. The poor, I hear, use what is called a "quick tub"—a tub of pine held together with hoops of bamboo. The body is placed into the box or tub **in the traditional sitting position**.

Small banners and ornaments decorated the house door. Two men came and presented a lacquered bowl of water and a white silk scarf. They were dressed in blue, with garments that looked like wings worn over it. Then we went into a large room with some gorgeously painted folding screens. The coffin sat at the end of the room under a white canopy. Six priests, dressed magnificently, sat on either side of the coffin. Two more knelt in front of a small altar.

The widow sat near the coffin. She was extremely beautiful dressed in a sky blue *kimono* with a fine white *haori*. Most family and friends wore blue or white silk, and **the room felt colorful and festive, rather than sad and gloomy**. Tea and sweets were passed around. Prayers were chanted and incense was burned. Then the procession to the cemetery began.

A priest carrying the *kaimiyo* tablet led the procession. Then came another priest carrying a lotus blossom. Ten priests followed, walking two-by-two and chanting prayers from books. Then came the

4人で運ばれてきました。美しくて、たいへん手入れの行き届いた墓地の浅い穴のなかへ、棺が納められました。墓穴が土で埋まるまで、お経は続きます。それからピンク色の蓮の花と、酒と豆とお菓子を載せた漆塗りのお盆が、新しい墓の上に置かれます。するとみんなは家に帰り、未亡人もひとりで歩いて帰っていきました。葬儀は始めから終わりまで、**きわめて厳粛で丁重な**ものでした。

coffin on a platform carried by four men. The coffin was put into a shallow hole in a beautiful, extremely well kept cemetery. Prayers were said until the hole was filled with dirt. A pink lotus plant and a lacquer tray holding *sake*, beans, and sweets was placed on top of the new grave. Then everyone went home, the widow walking home alone. The whole service was **extremely solemn and respectful**.

久保田にて
7月23日

　久保田へは船で到着しました。雄物川(おもの)を9時間旅して着いたのですが、もし陸の旅なら丸2日かかっていたことでしょう！

　久保田は秋田県の県庁所在地で、人口36,000人のとても魅力的な町です。太平山(たいへいざん)という立派な山が、肥沃な谷の上にそびえています。久保田には、ほかの城下町のような廃(すた)れたようすはありません。おもに織物を商い、広大で居心地のいい郊外が広がっています。きれいな家は木々に囲まれ、どこの庭にもそれぞれ門が造られています。どうやら健やかな中流階級の家庭があるようです。外国の影響はほとんどありません。

　ここでは、日本人医師が設立した立派な病院を訪れて、とても感銘を受けました。院長と6人の医師が出迎えてくれ、全員が和服——高価な絹の袴——を着ているのを見て、わたしはうれしくなりました。事務所でお茶をいただきましたが、そこでは6人の事務員が働いていました。それから病院施設のなかを案内してくれました。何もかもが**イギリスの水準を満たす**ほど清潔です。カヤバシ医師が、外科患者の重傷を治療するようすを見せてくれました。ここには目の病気が多いと医師は言います。原因は、家に人が多すぎること、通気が悪いこと、生活が貧しいこと、光が不

Kubota
July 23

We arrived in Kubota by boat. Traveling by the Omono River brought us here in nine hours, while it would have taken us two whole days on land!

Kubota, the capital of Akita-ken, is a very attractive town of 36,000 people. A fine mountain called Taiheisan rises above the fertile valley. Kubota does not have that dead look of other castle towns. It trades mainly in textiles, and it has a large, comfortable suburban area. Pretty houses are surrounded by trees, and each garden has its own gate. It seems there is quite a healthy middle class here. There's hardly any foreign influence at all.

I was impressed by a fine hospital organized by Japanese doctors that I visited here. The director and staff of six doctors met us, and I was delighted to see that they were all wearing national dress—rich silk *hakama*. We had tea in the management room where six clerks were working. Then they took us on a tour of the facilities. Everything was clean **enough to meet English standards**. Dr. Kayabashi let me watch as a surgical patient had severe wounds treated. Eye cases are common here, the doctors say, because of

十分なことだそうです。

　そのあと事務所へ戻って、イギリス風の食事と、受け皿とスプーン付きのカップでコーヒーをいただきました。この訪問は、ことのほかおもしろいものでした。

秋田の農家
Akita Farm-House

overcrowding, poor ventilation, poor living, and bad light.

Afterwards, we went back to the management room and had an English-style meal, with coffee cups and plates with spoons. I found this visit extremely interesting.

久保田にて
7月23日

　次に訪問したのは絹織物工場で、ここでは180人が手織り機で布を織っています。職工の半分は女たちでした。**婦人や少女に新しい仕事の機会がある**ことは、この国が社会改革へ向かうのに重要な助けとなるはずです。

　そのあとで、コンデンスミルクを買いに店へ行きました。店ですわっているあいだ、わたしのそばに集まった人混みのせいで、とても暑くて気分が悪くなりました。するといきなり警官がやってきて、人々に後ろへ下がって場所を空けるように言いました。そして、プライバシーを保てなくて申し訳ないという、署長からの伝言を届けてくれました。また、これからの滞在期間中、ふたりの警官がわたしに付き添って、人々を追い払ってくれると言うのです。わたしは心から感謝しました。警官たちのおかげで、ここでの残りの日々を快適に過ごせたのです。

　日本の警察には、全部で23,300人の教育を受けた男たちがいます。**彼らは士族の階級です。**人々にはとても穏やかに接します——ひとことふたこと静かに言うか、手を振るだけで、たいていはみんなおとなしくなるのです。5,000人以上が江戸、1,004人が京都、815人が大阪に配置されています。そして残りの10,000人は全国に散らばってい

Kubota
July 23

My next visit was to a silk factory, where 180 people weave on handlooms. Half of the employees were women. I believe **these new job opportunities for women and girls** are important to help move the country toward social reform.

Afterwards, I went to a store to buy some condensed milk. While I was sitting in the shop, I felt very hot and uncomfortable from the crowd that had gathered close around me. Suddenly, a policeman came and told the people to step back and give me room. He also delivered a message from the chief of police apologizing for the lack of privacy. He said for the rest of my stay, two policemen would escort me and keep the crowds away. I was very thankful, and the rest of my time here has been comfortable because of them.

The entire police force of Japan consists of 23,300 educated men. **They belong to the samurai class**. They are very gentle to the people—a few quiet words or a wave of the hand is usually enough to restore order. More than 5,000 of them are stationed at Yedo, 1,004 at Kiyoto, and 815 at Osaka. The remaining 10,000

ます。
　わたしは、久保田の町が日本のほかの町より好きになりました。それは、この町がまったく日本風なのに、衰退した雰囲気がないからかもしれません。

are spread around the country.

I think I like Kubota better than any other Japanese town. This may be because it is so completely Japanese, and it doesn't have that air of decay.

久保田にて
7月23日

いつまでも続く大雨のせいで、まだ久保田にいます。

これまで、伊藤のことについて、ほとんど話してきませんでしたね。彼ほどよい使用人兼通訳は望めないと思います。わたしは、あらゆる点で彼に頼っているのです。毎晩のように、時計、パスポート、お金の半分を伊藤に預けています。**もし彼が夜のうちにそれらを持って逃げてしまったら、わたしはどうしたらいいかわからないでしょう。**

でも、伊藤はよい少年とはいえません——外国人が大嫌いで、言うことを聞かないことがよくあるし、高慢になりがちなのです。それでも、けっして時間に遅れないし、夜は外出しないし、酒も飲まないし、指示を2度言う必要がありません。また、給料のほとんどを未亡人である母親に送っています。残りは煙草や砂糖菓子を買ったり、しょっちゅう髪を洗いにいったりするのに使っているようです。

伊藤はこの旅を始めたとき、まずまずの**英語**を話していましたが、いまではどんな通訳官よりも上手に話します。「俗語」と、正しい英語の区別にたいへん注意を払っています。英語と日本語の両方で日記をつけ、ときどきわたしに読んで聞かせますが、**とても細かく観察していることがわかります。**

伊藤がもっとも強く抱いているものは愛国心に違いあり

Kubota
July 23

We are still here in Kubota because of heavy, unstopping rain.

So far, I've said very little about Ito. I don't think I could have asked for a better servant or interpreter. I depend on him in almost every way. Every night he holds my watch, passport, and half of my money. **I don't know what I would do if he were to run away with them in the night**.

But Ito is not a good boy—he dislikes foreigners, he is often disagreeable, and he can be boastful. But he is never late, never goes out at night, never drinks *sake*, and never has to be told something twice. He sends most of his wages to his mother, a widow. The rest of it he seems to spend on tobacco, sweetmeats, and frequent shampooing.

Ito **spoke decent English** when we started this trip, and now he speaks better than any official interpreter. He is very careful to distinguish between "slang" and proper English. He keeps a diary in both English and Japanese, which he reads to me sometimes, **revealing some very detailed observation**.

I believe his strongest feeling is patriotism. He is

ません。日本をとても誇りに思い、教養のない人たちを嫌っているのです。また、夕食用に鶏か何かの肉を手に入れようとして失敗した話を、毎晩のように聞かせて笑わせてくれます。

very proud of Japan and dislikes uneducated people. He amuses me almost every night with stories of his unsuccessful attempts to get chicken or any kind of meat for dinner.

久保田にて

7月25日

　宿屋の主人はとてもやさしい人で、姪の結婚式にわたしも招待してくれました。その儀式は、**本で読んだ日本の結婚式とは違うものでした**。どうやら士族階級と平民階級とでは、儀式に違いがあるようです。

　嫁入り道具と家具が、朝早くに花婿の家へ運ばれました。嫁入り道具のなかには、たくさんの絹と衣装が入っています。6バレルの日本酒と、7種類の香辛料もありました。家具は、漆塗りの木の枕がふたつ、木綿と絹のふとんが数枚、絹のざぶとん数枚、漆塗りの箱、糸車、おひつ、しゃもじ、飾りのついた鉄瓶ふたつ、漆塗りの飯椀が数個、銅のたらいがふたつ、手ぬぐい数枚、煙草盆がふたつ、そしてさまざまな台所道具です。

　花婿は22歳で、花嫁は17歳でした。花嫁はとてもきれいな娘さんです。真っ白な絹の着物を着て、顔にはおしろいを塗り、頭から足まで覆う白い布をかぶっています。花嫁は花婿の家まで乗り物で運ばれ、そのあとから両親と友人がついていきました。誰もが提灯を手にしていました。

Kubota
July 25

The house-master of my *yadoya* was kind enough to get me an invitation to his niece's wedding. The ceremony was **not like the Japanese wedding ceremonies I've read about in books**. Apparently there is a difference in ceremonies between the samurai and *heimin* class.

The trousseau and furniture were carried to the bridegroom's house early in the morning. Inside the trousseau were piles of silk and clothes. There were also six barrels of *sake* and seven different kinds of condiments. The furniture consisted of two lacquered, wooden pillows, some cotton and silk *futons*, a few silk cushions, a lacquer box, a spinning-wheel, a rice bucket and ladle, two ornamental iron kettles, some lacquer rice bowls, two copper basins, a few towels, two *tabako-bons*, and various kitchen utensils.

The bridegroom was twenty-two, and the bride was seventeen. The bride was very pretty. She was dressed all in white silk and her face was painted white. She wore a white veil that covered her from head to foot. She was carried to the bridegroom's house in a *norimon*, followed by her parents and

宿屋の主人とわたしが到着したとき、花婿は大きな部屋の前のほうにすわっていました。花婿の家族全員が片側にすわり、花嫁の家族が反対側にすわっています。ふたりの美しい少女が花嫁を連れて入ってきました。花嫁は花婿の前に向かい合ってすわりました。漆塗りの小さな膳がふたりのあいだに置かれました。その上には、注ぎ口がふたつついた銚子に酒を満たしたもの、とっくり、盃が載っています。それから料理を載せた膳が客たちの前にひとつずつ置かれ、みんなで食べはじめました。

　このあと、花婿の父親と、花婿の母親、そして花嫁のあいだで、**酒を飲む儀式**が行われました。やがてごはんと魚が運ばれました。さらに酒を飲む儀式があり、つぎに汁物が出されました。最後に、新婚夫妻が両口の銚子から酒を飲みました。これは、**夫婦が人生の喜びと悲しみをともに味わうことを象徴している**のです。

　これで結婚の儀式は終わり、残りの招待客がなかへ招かれました。彼らはごちそうを食べたり酒を飲んだりしましたが、すべてがとても丁寧で上品でした。どんなささいなことでも、何世紀も続いた様式に従い、伝統にのっとって行われるのです。儀式そのものを除けば、**結婚式はだらだらと長くて、どこかもの悲しい行事でした。**

friends. Everyone carried a Chinese lantern.

When the house-master and I arrived, the bridegroom was seated at the front of a large room. All of the bridegroom's family sat on one side and the bride's on the other. Two beautiful girls brought in the bride. She sat in front of the bridegroom, facing him. A little lacquered table was placed between them. On it was a two-spouted kettle full of *sake*, some *sake* bottles, and some cups. Then a *zen* loaded with food was placed before each guest, and we all ate.

After this, there was **ceremonial *sake* drinking** among the father of the groom, the mother of the groom, and the bride. Then rice and fish were brought in. There was more ceremonial drinking, then soup was served. Finally, the newly married couple drank *sake* from the two-spouted kettle. This is **symbolic of the couple tasting the joys and sorrows of life together**.

This was the end of the wedding ceremony, and the rest of the wedding guests were invited in. They feasted and drank, but everything was very polite and proper. Every detail was done according to tradition, the way it had been for centuries. Except for the ceremony itself, I found **the wedding to be a rather long and melancholy event**.

鶴形にて
7月27日

　天気が回復したので、旅を続けることにしました。近くにある、港という町で祭りがあるので、道は行き来する人でごった返していました。

　港の町では、大通りに沿って祭りが繰り広げられていました。神明という神【訳注：天照大神】を称える祭りです。敷物をした縁台や桟敷で人々がすわったり、酒を飲んだり、人混みを見おろしたりしていました。そのそばでは猿や犬が芸をしています。また、2匹の羊と1匹の豚を見ようと人だかりができていました。日本のこの地域では見かけない動物なのです。40人の男たちが、寺のような屋根のついた車（曳山）を引き、その上で上流階級の子どもたちが踊っています。そばの舞台では、古めかしい衣装を着たふたりの男が、とてもゆっくりした単調な舞を踊っていました。ふたりは奇妙なポーズをして、ときどき足を踏み鳴らし、しわがれた声で「ノー」というような言葉をしょっちゅう発するのです。

　町でいちばん混み合っているところでは、ふたつの大きな曳山が、それぞれ200人の男たちに引かれていました。曳山は重い角材で作られ、長さ30フィート、高さは50フィートあります。それぞれに8つの巨大な車輪がついています。曳山の前部では30人の楽師が、なんともすさ

Tsugurata
July 27

With improved weather, we continued on our way. There was a *matsuri* in the nearby town of Minato, so the roads were full of people coming and going.

In Minato, **the *matsuri* stretched along the main street**. The festival honored the god Shimmai. There were covered platforms and places for people to sit, drink, and watch the crowds below, and nearby there were performing monkeys and dogs. People crowded around to see two sheep and a pig, which are unknown animals in this part of Japan. I watched forty men pulling a cart with a roof like a temple, on which children of the highest class were dancing. On a stage nearby, two men in antique clothes were performing a very slow, dull dance. They held strange postures and occasionally stamped their foot, often saying something that sounded like "No" in a hoarse voice.

In the most crowded part of town, there were two great *matsuri* carts pulled by two hundred men each. The carts were made of heavy beams and were thirty feet long by fifty feet high. Each had eight huge wheels. In the front of the car, thirty musicians were

まじい音のする音楽を奏でています。側面には、聖なる山と、鬼を退治する神道の神の絵が描かれていました。

　盛岡やこの地方のほかの村で気づいたのですが、**塀に囲まれた大きくて裕福そうな家があれば、それはたいてい造り酒屋なのです**。酒を示す看板は、玄関の外に飾られた木の枝を丸くまとめたもの（杉玉）です。同じような看板が、かつてイギリスでもワインの店を示すのに使われていたのは、なんと不思議なことでしょう。

playing the most awful-sounding music. On the sides there were representations of a scared mountain and of the Shinto gods killing demons.

At Morioka and other villages in this region, I noticed that **if you see a large, wealthy-looking, fenced-in house, it is usually a *sake* brewer's house.** The sign for *sake* is a round bush that is kept outside the door. How strange that the same symbol was also used in England to signal the sale of wine.

大館にて
7月29日

　背中がとても痛いので、1日に7、8マイルしか進めません。馬に乗るときは、自分の鞍を使ってみて、それから日本の鞍を使いますが、**結局いつも歩くことになります**。行かなければならないから、進んでいるだけという状況です。北日本を旅するのは、身体が丈夫な人だけにしたほうがよさそうです。

　雨はやみそうにありません。そのせいで健康がすぐれず、この国の全体的な印象も悪くなりそうです。いつも衣服がぬれたままで過ごしています。荷物もぜんぶぬれて、ここに持ってきた油紙の雨ガッパも役に立ちません。

　次の目的地、小繋には舟で着きました。川が荒れて、危険な船旅でした。豪雨のため、政府が渡し舟を全部止めたと言われました。でも、**これまでに何度も同じように言われたことがあって、いつも嘘だったのです**。そこで、降りしきる雨のなかを馬に乗って、舟を探しに川まで行ってみました。すると川岸には、渡河を禁じるという政府からの触れ書きがありました。がっかりしましたが、ちょうどそのとき、1艘の舟が川を渡ってきたのです。わたしたちが大声で船頭に呼びかけると、小繋に行くところだとわかりました——わたしたちの目的地ではありませんか！　なかなかたいへんでしたが、やっとのことで舟に乗りこむこと

Odate
July 29

I have been suffering so much from pain in my spine that I cannot travel more than seven or eight miles a day. When I ride a horse, I try using my own saddle, then a Japanese saddle, but **I usually end up walking**. I only go on because I have to go on. Only strong people should travel in northern Japan.

The rain will not stop. I know it is affecting my health, as well as my general impressions of this country. I live in wet clothes. All of my luggage is wet, and the oiled-paper rain cloak I bought here does not help.

We got to Kotsunagi, our next destination, by boat. It was a dangerous ride on a wild river. The rain has been so heavy that we were told the government had prohibited all travel by river. But **I had been told similar things many times before, and they had always been false**. We rode horses in the pouring rain to the river to see for ourselves. There, on the shore, was a government order prohibiting boat travel. My heart sank, but just then, a boat came rushing over the river. We yelled to the boatmen and discovered they were going to Kotsunagi—our destination! With

ができました。とはいえ、とても恐ろしい船旅でした。船頭たちが、あまりの重労働に死んでしまうのではないかと思ったほどです。また、途中で屋形船を見かけました。7人の船頭が必死で船を操ろうとしていましたが、**ひとりが船から落ちてしまったのです。**そして、もう2度と姿を見ることはありませんでした。わたしは今も、**その人の家族に思いを馳せています。**あとで伊藤に、そのような危険のなかでどう感じたか尋ねてみました。すると、「わたしはずっと母親に孝行してきたし、正直だったから、いいところへ行けますようにと願っていたのです」と答えました。

今朝、伊藤がわたしを起こして、旅人たちから聞いた噂話を伝えてくれました。首相が暗殺され、50人の警官が殺されたというのです！* この地方には、途方もない政治的な噂がたくさん流れています。この10年でさまざまな変化があったので、**人々が政府を信頼できないのも無理はありません。**

*この噂はおそらく、近衛部隊の一部による反乱が間違って伝えられたのでしょう。その反乱のことは、あとで蝦夷に着いてから知りました。

蓑笠姿
Straw Rain-Cloak

some difficulty, we managed to get on the boat. But it was a frightening ride. I thought the boatmen would kill themselves from working so hard. On the way, we saw a houseboat. Seven boatmen were trying to control it, but **one man fell overboard**. We never saw him again. **My heart goes out to his family**. Later, I asked Ito how he felt to be in such danger. He said, "I've been good to my mother, and honest. I hoped I would go to a good place."

This morning, Ito woke me with a rumor he heard from some travelers. They said the Prime Minister had been assassinated, and fifty policemen had been killed!* There are many wild political rumors in this region. After the changes of the last ten years, **it's no wonder people don't feel confident in their government**.

*Note: This rumor was probably based on the partial rebellion of the Imperial Guard. I learned about this later when I landed in Yezo.

白沢にて
7月29日

　ついに雨がやみ、日が照って、田舎はまたすばらしい景色になりました。日本は太陽が輝くと、まるで天国のようになります。600マイルの道中、日光を浴びても美しくないところは、この国でほとんど見たことがありません。

　わたしたちは、ほろ酔いかげんの馬子に馬を引かれて旅を続けました。温めた酒の効果はおもしろいものです。これを飲むと酔ってにぎやかになりますが、とても楽しそうなのです。これまでたくさんの酔っ払いを見ましたが、ひとりとして怒ったり、けんか腰になったりしませんでした。
　わたしの宿泊代（伊藤の分も含めて）は、1日3シリングもかかりません。**しょっちゅうへんぴな村落に泊まることを考えれば、宿は驚くほど良質です**（蚤とひどい臭いを無視できればですが）。同じくらいへんぴなら、世界じゅうのどの宿よりも日本の宿のほうがいいでしょう。

　今夜も男たちは仕事から帰ってきました。ほかの何千という村の男たちと同じです。彼らは食べ、煙草を吸い、子どもたちと遊び、縄を編み、わらじを作り、竹を割り、蓑をこしらえていました。イギリスの男たちのように居酒屋で集まったりはしません。家は貧しいかもしれませんが、日本の男たちは暮らしを楽しんでいます。イギリスの労働

Shirasawa
July 29

It finally stopped raining, the sun is shining, and the countryside is glorious again. When Japan gets sunshine, it turns into paradise. In 600 miles, I have rarely seen any patch of country that wouldn't look beautiful in the sunlight.

We continued on our way with a slightly drunk *mago* leading our horses. The effects of hot *sake* are interesting: it creates a noisy but happy kind of drunk. I have seen many drunk people now, but none of them have been angry or aggressive.

My hotel expenses (including Ito's) are less than 3s. a day. **Considering that I often stay in remote hamlets**, the accommodation has been surprisingly good (if you ignore the fleas and bad smells). They are probably better than accommodations I could find in equally remote regions elsewhere in the world.

Tonight, the men came home from their work just as they do in thousands of other villages. They ate, smoked, played with their children, twisted straw ropes, made straw sandals, cut bamboo, and wove straw raincoats. The men do not gather at the *sake* shop like the men of England do. Although their

者階級の家でよくあるような争いごとは、ここでは起こりません。誰もが従順という決まりを守って暮らしているのです。

　日本人は多くの点でイギリス人より優れていると思います。ただし、ほかの点ではかなり劣っていますが。この礼儀正しく、働き者で、文化的な人々と一緒に住んでいると、彼らの作法とわたしたちの作法を比べるべきではないということを、つい忘れてしまいそうになります。**わたしたちは何世紀もキリスト教による恩恵を受けているのです**から、比べるのは不当でしょう。それでもなお、わたしたちイギリス人がこの比較で優位に立てないこともあるのです！

　7月30日——わたしの隣の部屋には、江戸の近くの目黒不動尊へ巡礼に行く、ふたりの男が泊まっています。彼らは頭を丸め、長い数珠をかけて、小さな太鼓を叩きながら歩きます。今朝は5時から勤行を始めました。それは、「南無妙法蓮華経」という言葉を2時間繰り返すことです。この言葉の意味については、**最高の学者たちでさえ意見が分かれて**いるのです。

homes may be poor, Japanese men enjoy them. The fighting that often occurs in English working-class homes does not happen here. **Everyone lives by rules of obedience**.

I think Japanese are superior to us English in many ways. But they are very much behind us in other ways. Living among these polite, hardworking, civilized people, I often forget that I shouldn't compare their manners with ours, because **we've had the benefit of many centuries of Christianity**. Even so, sometimes we English do not come out ahead in these comparisons!

July 30—In the room next to mine are two men who are on a pilgrimage to the shrine of Fudo at Megura, near Yedo. They have shaved heads and long rosaries. They beat small drums as they walk. They began praying this morning at five o'clock. Their prayers consisted of repeating *Namu miyo ho ren ge kiyo* for two hours. **Even the best scholars have different opinions** as to what these words mean.

青森県、碇ヶ関にて
8月2日

　わたしたちの困難はますますひどくなるばかりです。雨は6日間もやみません。ひどい嵐のせいで、碇ヶ関で足止めになっているのです。何もかもが湿り、カビが生えて緑色です——服、ベッド、シーツ、かばん、本、そしてブーツもです。津軽海峡はすぐそこなのに、行くことができません。土地の人たちは神々に、この異常な雨からお守りください、と祈っています。

　一昨日は、旅のなかでもっとも興味深い日でした。雨がやみそうだったので、わたしたちは正午に白沢を出発しました。みごとな杉の木に囲まれて、美しい景色でした。でも、雨のせいで小川も大きな川もひどく増水したため、ほとんど渡ることができません。**山では、泥流や土砂崩れが起こっていました。**丸太や根こそぎ抜けた木が、川を流れ下っていきます。そして秋田県と青森県の県境の峠で、ついに嵐が始まったのです。道は洗い流されてなくなったり、倒木や落石で完全に遮られたりしました。**渡るはずの橋も流されました。**たいへんな事態になったと思いましたが、3人の馬子は手馴れていて勇敢でした。わたしを荷馬にくくりつけると、川の浅瀬を何度も渡っていくのです。馬子たちは肩まで水に浸かっていました。馬が上り下りできるよう、斧を使って土手に踏み段を刻むのですが、激しい雨のせいですぐに流されてしまいます。そのため馬がひどく

Ikarigaseki, Aomori-ken
August 2

Our difficulties have become greater. The rain hasn't stopped in six days. I've been stuck in Ikarigaseki because of terrible storms. Everything is either wet or green with mildew—my clothes, bed, sheets, bag, books, and boots. We are so close to the Tsugaru Strait, but we cannot go. The local people are calling on the gods to save them from these unnatural rains.

The day before yesterday was the most interesting of my journey. We left Shirasawa at noon because it looked like it would stop raining. The scenery was beautiful, with glorious cedar trees all around. But the rain had made the streams and rivers so wild that it was almost impossible to cross. **There were mudslides and landslides on the mountains**. Logs and entire trees came rushing down the rivers. Then, at the top of the pass that separates Akita and Aomori-ken, it began to storm. The roads were either washed away or totally blocked by fallen trees and rocks. **A bridge we needed to cross had been washed** away. Things began to look very bad, but our three *mago* were skilled and brave. They tied me to the pack-horse and we forded the river many times. The *mago* were up to their

よろめくので、わたしは一度落馬して頭を打ちました。最後に渡った川はあまりに荒れ狂っていたので、怖くて思わず目をつぶってしまいました！

　雨はほとんどの田畑を台なしにしました——田んぼは洪水になり、作物がすべて流されたのです。わたしたちは平川(ひらかわ)にかかる大きな橋をふたつ渡って、とうとう碇ヶ関に着きました。

　わたしは疲れ果てて、薄暗い宿屋で床に入りましたが、伊藤に起こされました。さっき渡ったばかりのふたつの橋が落ちそうだと言うのです！　雨の降るなか、伊藤と一緒に川岸へ走っていくと、村じゅうの人が集まっていました。あらゆる形の残骸が川を流れていくのを、じっと見守りました。すると、長さ30フィートの巨大な丸太が、何本か流れてくるのに気づきました。ひとつ目の橋の一部です！橋が落ちたに違いありません！　この大きな丸太がふたつ目の橋にぶつかり、ふたつ目の橋も轟音を立てて崩れ落ちました。**今やこの地域の村は以前よりさらに孤立してしまい**、わたしたちは川が落ち着いて浅瀬を渡れるようになるまで、ここに足止めとなったのです。

　つづき——以下は、この村での時間のつぶし方です。まず1日に3回、川の水位がどれくらい下がったか見にいきます。そして本を読んだり、子どもたちを見たり、宿の主人と話したりします。目が痛いという数人の村人には、1日3回亜鉛ローションを塗ってあげます。台所で料理のよ

shoulders in water. Using axes, they cut stairs out of the riverbanks for the horses, but the rain came down so hard the stairs quickly got washed out. The horses stumbled so much that once I fell off and hit my head. The river was so wild at our last crossing that I admit I closed my eyes from fear!

The rain had destroyed most farms—the rice fields were flooded and all the crops were washed away. We finally reached Ikarigaseki by crossing the Hirakawa on two large bridges.

I was exhausted and went to bed at our gloomy *yadoya*, but Ito woke me with the news that the two bridges we had just crossed were falling down! In the pouring rain, Ito and I rushed to the riverbank where the whole village had gathered. We watched as all kinds of debris came rushing down the river. Then we noticed several huge pieces of timber, thirty feet long, rushing down. These were pieces of the first bridge! It must have collapsed! These massive logs crashed into the second bridge, and the second bridge fell down with a roar. **Now the villages in this region are even more isolated than they were before**, and we are stuck here until the river goes down enough to ford.

Continued—This is how I pass the time in this village: I go out three times a day to see how low the river has gotten. I read, watch the children, and talk with the house-master. I apply zinc lotion to several villagers with sore eyes three times a day. I watch the

うすを観察したり、やはり台所にいる馬に会いにいきます。そして、青森へ行くためのあらゆる手段を考えるのです。

　今日の午後はいい天気で風があったので、男の子たちが凧をあげました。凧は四角い形で、竹の枠に紙を貼って作ります。そのほとんどに歴史上の人物の顔が描かれています。ふたつの凧のあいだで、おもしろい競争がありました。**凧の糸に砕いたガラスをたくさん貼りつけて、お互いに相手の糸を切ろうとするのです。**ひとりがついに成功し、相手の凧を勝ち取りました。また、竹馬に乗って凧をあげている少年たちもいました。それから竹馬の競争があり、多くの子どもたちが参加していました。

cooking in the *daidokoro*, and I visit the horses, which are also in the *daidokoro*. I study every possible route to Aomori.

This afternoon was fine and windy, so the boys flew kites. They are rectangular and made of paper on a bamboo frame. Almost all are decorated with the face of a historical figure. There was an interesting contest between two kites: **the strings were covered with broken glass, and each boy tried to cut the string of the other**. When one finally succeeded, he got to keep the other kite. There were also boys who flew their kites while walking on stilts. Then there was a stilt race, in which many children participated.

黒石にて
8月5日

　黒石という、人口5,500人の町に2日間泊まります。部屋は風通しがよく快適で、ここならよく休めそうです。

　青森では情報を得るのが困難です。この地方では、**ほんの数マイル離れたところで起きていることでも、誰も何も知らないのです。**郵便局でさえ、青森と函館を結ぶ郵便船がいつ出るのかわかりません。

　今日の夕方、目を見張るような光景を見ました。七夕、もしくは星夕という祭りです。今週のあいだ毎晩7時から10時まで、町のあらゆる通りを行列が練り歩くのです。男たちが2本の柱で支えた箱を肩にかついでいきます。箱のなかには、村人の願いごとを書いた紙切れが入っています。高さ20フィートくらいの大きな提灯があり、それには伝説上の獣が描かれています。そのまわりを囲んでいるのは、いろいろな形——魚、扇、鳥、凧、太鼓——の提灯をさげた何百という人々です。行列には太鼓も出ていて、小さな太鼓もあれば、人の背丈ほどの大きな太鼓もあります。提灯がふわふわと漂っていき、それを持っている人が闇のなかへ消えていくのですが、**これほど幻想的な光景は見たことがありません。**わたしは伊藤に、この祭りにどういう意味があるのか訊いてみましたが、説明するのは難し

Kuroishi
August 5

I am staying two days in Kuroishi, a town of 5,500 people. My room is airy and cheerful, and I am resting well here.

It is difficult to get any information on Aomori. In this region, **nobody knows about anything happening only a few miles away.** Even at the Post Office they cannot tell me when the mail boat sails between Aomori and Hakodate.

This evening, I saw a spectacular sight. It is the time of the *tanabata* or *seiseki* festival. During this week, a parade passes through all the streets of town from 7 to 10 p.m. every night. The men carry an ark on two poles on their shoulders. In it are slips of paper with the villagers' wishes written on them. There is a large lantern, about 20 feet high, with mythical beasts painted on it, and all around it are hundreds of people carrying lanterns of different shapes—fish, fans, birds, kites, drums. Drumming accompanies the parade, both on small drums and drums nearly as tall as a man. **I never saw anything more like a fairy scene**, with the lanterns floating by and their carriers disappearing into the shadows. I tried to ask Ito what

いと思ったようで、「サトウさんなら、ぜんぶ説明できるでしょうけれど」などと言います。

it all means, but he finds it difficult to explain. He says, "Mr. Satow **would be able to tell you all about it**."

黒石にて
8月5日

　清潔で風通しがいいこと以外に、ここの部屋のよいところは、隣の家が見おろせることです。今日は、若い娘さんが自分の結婚式の準備をしているのを見ることができたのです！

　髪の結い方がとてもおもしろいものでした。**まさに芸術作品です**。まず頭頂部の髪を3つの房に分けます。真ん中の房をよくとかして、サネカズラで作ったびんづけ油で固め、2インチあげます。それから後ろに折り返して結び、髪の後ろ側へピンで止めます。残りの房は両側から後ろへとかして、紙の撚り糸で結びます。偽物の髪で作った毛束（かもじ）を、後頭部にピンで止めます。髪でいくつかの輪型やアーチ型を作り、金をちりばめた藍色の縮緬を編み込みます。そして1本のべっ甲のかんざしが、唯一の装飾品として飾られます。

　こめかみやうなじの遅れ毛は、ぜんぶ毛抜きで注意深く抜き、眉もすべて落とします。顔におしろいを塗り、歯を黒く染め直し、下唇に紅を塗ります。それから、とても美しくて上品な、日本の女物の着物を身につけます。この支度には全部で3時間かかりましたが、できあがると、花嫁は磨いた金属鏡をのぞきこみ、満足そうに微笑みました。

Kuroishi
August 5

Another good thing about my room here, aside from being clean and airy, is that it looks down into a neighbor's house. Today I was able to watch a young woman prepare for her wedding!

Her hair arrangement was most interesting. **It is a complete work of art**. The hair was divided into three sections on top of the head. The middle section was carefully combed, stiffened with dressing made of Uvario Japonica, and raised two inches. Then it was turned back, tied, and pinned to the back of the hair. The rest was combed from each side to the back and tied with twine made of paper. A chignon made of fake hair was pinned to the back of the head. Several loops and bows of hair were added, interwoven with dark-blue crepe splashed with gold. A single tortoise-shell comb was added as the only ornament.

All the small hairs at the temples and the neck were carefully pulled out with tweezers. Her eyebrows were also removed. The woman painted her face white and reblackened her teeth. A patch of red was put on her bottom lip. Then she was dressed in the exquisitely good taste of Japanese female dress.

今日そのあとで、3人のキリスト教徒の学生がやってきました。彼らはみな、弘前という、近くの城下町の出身です。3人の若い紳士は非常に聡明そうで、英語を少し話せました。そして、30人の人々を**キリスト教に導いた**と話していました。

婦人の鏡
A Lady's Mirror

All of this took three hours, and at the end, the bride looked into a polished metal mirror and smiled with satisfaction.

Later today, three Christian students visited me. They were all from Hirosaki, a nearby castle town. The three young gentlemen looked extremely intelligent and they all spoke a little English. They told me they had **helped** thirty people **embrace Christianity**.

黒石にて

　昨日はすばらしい天気だったので、伊藤を連れずに、人力車でその地方を見てまわりました。とても楽しいときを過ごしました。風景は美しく、青、緑、群青色、藍色など、さまざまな色合いを見せていました。いくつかの村を通りすぎましたが、そこでは農家の人たちが窓のない土の家に住んでいました。家の片側で家畜を飼い、反対側に人が住むのです。これらの農家にはよい馬がたくさんいて、作物もみごとなものでした。それほど貧しくないに違いありません。きっと祭りの日には、すばらしい着物を着てやってくるのでしょう。
　上中野(かみなかの)はとても美しいところで、下中野(しもなかの)には温泉があります。その町は、ほとんどが茶屋や、宿屋、公衆浴場ばかりです。人々は浴場でも、ほかの場所にいるときと同じように礼儀正しくふるまいます。手ぬぐいやひしゃくを渡すときも、とても深くお辞儀をするのです。**浴場では政治的な議論が行われ、世論が形成される**とのことです。これは日本の大きな特色といえるでしょう。

Kuroishi

Yesterday was beautiful, and I took a *kuruma* to explore the region without Ito. I had a pleasant time. The beautiful scenery was all different shades of blue, green, cobalt, and indigo. We passed through several villages where farmers live in mud houses with no windows. The animals lived in one side of the house while the people lived in the other. These farmers owned many good horses and their crops were splendid. They must not be very poor. I'm sure on festival days they call come out wearing wonderful clothes.

Upper Nakano is very beautiful, and Lower Nakano has hot springs. The town is mostly tea-houses, *yadoyas*, and public bath-houses. People are just as polite in the bath-house as they are everywhere else. They pass towels and water dippers with very deep bows. I hear that **bath-houses are where politics are discussed and public opinion is formed**. It is an important feature of Japan.

5章

函館から平取へ
(北海道) 　　(北海道)

From Hakodate to Biratori

蝦夷、函館にて
1878年、8月

　黒石から青森まで、たいへんな旅でした。再び雨が降りはじめたうえに、塩漬けの魚を運ぶ何百頭もの荷馬のせいで、道が泥沼のようになっていたのです。でも浪岡で、この旅の最後の峠を越えると、ついに暗い灰色の海を見おろすことができました。これこそ青森湾で、その向こうが津軽海峡です。わたしの長い陸の旅も、もうすぐ終わるのです！　ある旅人から、函館行きの船が今夜出ると聞いたので、4人の男を雇い、泥のなかを引いたり、押したり、持ちあげたりしてもらって、なんとか青森に着きました。

　三菱の事務所で船の切符を買いましたが、船が出るまでわずか30分しかありませんでした。青森は、灰色の砂浜の上に灰色の家がある町です。でも、**松が生い茂るまわりの丘や、泥炭の匂いがする大地は、わたしの故郷を思い出させます。**

　蒸気船は70トンの少し古い船でした。ヨットのようにきれいで、すっきりしていましたが、やはりヨットと同じく悪天候には不向きです。船に乗ると、また雨が降りだしました。船長も船員たちも日本人で英語は話せませんが、とても親切です。服がぬれたので、夜じゅう寒いのではないかと不安でしたが、船長が数枚の毛布を掛けてくれました。

Hakodate, Yezo
August, 1878

We've had a difficult journey from Kuroishi to Aomori. The rains began again, and hundreds of pack-horses transporting salted fish had turned the roads into mud. But as we crossed our very last mountain ridge at Namioka, I looked down at a dark grey sea. This was Aomori Bay, and beyond it was Tsugaru Strait. My long land journey was almost over! A traveler we met said the boat for Hakodate was leaving that night, so I hired four men to drag, push, and lift me through the mud to reach Aomori.

We bought our boat tickets at the Mitsu Bishi office and only had half an hour before the boat departed. Aomori is a town of grey houses built on a beach of grey sand. But **the surrounding pine-covered hills and peat-smelling earth reminded me of home**.

The steamship was a little old boat of 70 tons. She was as clean and neat as a yacht, but like a yacht, she was not made for bad weather. As we boarded the boat, the rain started again. The captain and crew were Japanese and did not speak any English, but they were kind. My clothes were wet so I was afraid of being cold throughout the night, but the captain

早朝に出帆しましたが、そのときから風が強く吹いていました。11時には激しい強風になりました。あたり一面、水しぶきが高く荒々しくあがっています。船室には水がたくさん入ってきました。船長が気圧計を見に、30分おきに船室へ入ってきます。お茶に入れる砂糖をくれると、顔をしかめて、「ひどい天気ですね」という仕草をしました。船長は心配しているものの、**イギリス人と変わらないほど落ち着いているのです！**

　14時間も荒波に揺られたあと、函館港に到着しました。雨と風のなか、蝦夷の山々が暗い雲を背景にそびえています。「北の海の騒音」が、この海岸へやってきたわたしを荒々しく歓迎してくれました。寒くて薄暗いですが、なんとなく北国のようすにうれしくなり、故郷に帰ったような気がしました。

　今は聖公会の宣教師館にいます。ここに泊まるよう、デニング夫妻があたたかく迎えてくれたのです。わたしはぬれた泥だらけの服を着、手袋もブーツもぼろぼろで、ひどいありさまでした。でも、**ここに着くことができて、勝ち誇った気分です**。日本奥地の障害をすべて乗り越えて、**自分が予想していた以上のことを成し遂げた**のですから！

　海の音はなんて心地よいのでしょう！　屋根に当たる雨音は、我が家で聞く音のようです。震えるほどの寒ささえ、清々しくて気持ちいいのです！　鍵のついたドアと、簡易ベッドのかわりに本物のベッドのあることが、**どれほどうれしいか、あなたには想像もつかないでしょうね！**

covered me with several blankets.

We set sail in the early evening when there was a strong wind. By eleven, that wind turned into a gale. The water was high and rough all around us. Much water entered the cabin. The captain came into the cabin every half-hour to check the barometer. He offered me some sugar for my tea and made a face and gesture meaning "bad weather." The captain was worried, but **he showed as much calmness as a Briton**!

After fourteen hours of rough sailing, we reached Hakodate Harbor. It was windy and rainy, and the Yezo mountains rose against dark clouds. The "noises of the northern sea" gave me a wild welcome to these shores. It was cold and grey, but somehow I was pleased by the northern look and I felt like I was back home.

I am now at the Church Mission House, where Mr. and Mrs. Dening have kindly invited me to stay. I was a terrible sight, covered in wet, muddy clothing, with my ruined gloves and boots. But **I feel triumphant at having arrived here**. I've survived all the obstacles of Japan's interior, and **I've accomplished more than I thought I would**!

How musical the sound of the ocean is! The sound of the rain on the roof sounds like home. Even shivering from the cold feels refreshing and welcome! **You cannot imagine how delightful** it is to have a door with a lock and a bed instead of a cot!

蝦夷、函館にて
1878年8月13日

　2日間の暴風雨のあと、天気はすっかりよくなりました。ここの涼しい気候のほうが、本州の気候よりわたしは好きです。霧が晴れると、森の丘ではなく、裸の山が現れました——最近噴火したばかりの火山です。砂浜が湾を縁どり、海の水はアドリア海のように真っ青です。ジブラルタルを思わせる景色ですが、**再び西洋を見ているような気分になったとたん**、人力車が黄色い肌の小柄な車夫に引かれて通り過ぎ、日本にいるのだったと思い出すのです。

　函館は、通りは広くてきれいなのですが、家は薪の山に毛がはえた程度のものです。町全体がまるで一時しのぎの仮設のようで、屋根は重い石で押さえてあるのです。土や芝生で覆った屋根もあります。これはたぶん、家に火の粉が飛ばないようにしているのでしょう。

Hakodate, Yezo
August 13, 1878

After two days of rainstorms, the weather has turned very fine. I like the cooler weather here better than the weather on the mainland. When the fog lifts, it doesn't reveal forested hills but naked mountains—volcanoes that burned out only recently. Sandy beaches border the bay, and the water is as blue as the Adriatic. It reminds me of Gibraltar, **but as you start to think you're seeing the West again**, a *kuruma* passes with little yellow-skinned men pulling it, and you realize that you're in Japan.

In Hakodate, the streets are wide and clean, but the houses are little more than piles of wood. The whole town looks very temporary, with the roofs held down by heavy stones. Some roofs are covered with dirt and crops of grass. This is supposed to prevent houses from catching fire.

蝦夷、函館にて

　函館にいるのがとても楽しいので、一日一日と滞在を延ばしてしまいます！　でも明日には、北への長い旅を始めたいと思っています。

　残念なことに、昨日、伊藤**について不愉快なことがわかりました**。ここ函館で、以前伊藤を雇っていた植物学者のマリーズ氏に会ったのです。彼が言うには、じつはこの数か月間、伊藤は月7ドルでマリーズ氏のために働くと契約していたそうです。ところが、伊藤はわたしが12ドル払うと聞いて、こちらで働こうと逃げてきたのです！　マリーズ氏は伊藤がいないせいで、**たいへん困った**そうです。この少年はとても賢いうえに、植物を集めて乾かす方法も教えてあったからです。わたしはとても申し訳なく思い、自分との契約が終わったらすぐに本来のご主人に返します、と言いました。マリーズ氏はこれから1年半、中国と台湾に伊藤を連れていく予定です。

Hakodate, Yezo

I am enjoying Hakodate so much that I find myself staying longer, day by day! But, I hope to start my long tour of the north tomorrow.

I am sad to say **I discovered something unpleasant about** Ito yesterday. Here in Hakodate, I met Mr. Maries, the botanist who had hired Ito before. He said that Ito had actually been engaged to work with Mr. Maries these past few months for $7 a month. But, when Ito heard that I was offering $12, he ran away to work for me! Mr. Maries **has had a very hard time** without Ito, because the boy is very clever and he had been trained how to gather plants and dry them. I was very sorry, and I told Mr. Maries that as soon as Ito's contract with me has ended, he will be returned to his rightful master. Mr. Maries plans to take Ito with him to China and Formosa for the next year and a half.

蝦夷、
じゅんさい沼にて
8月17日

　わたしはまた未開の地にいます！　湖の上にせり出すように建てた家の外にすわっているのです。近くの丘を降りてくるのは、槍で熊を殺したばかりの男たちです。わたしは完全にひとりぼっちですが、とても清々しい気分です。伊藤を1日だけ函館に残し、ひとりで馬に乗ってここへやってきたのです。日本語の単語をいくつか並べて、1晩泊まる居心地のいい部屋と、ごはん、卵、豆の食事を手に入れました。まだ「**踏みならされた道**」からは外れていませんが、**日本の先住民であるアイヌの地**へ旅することに、わくわくしています。未開の北の地方は美しくて、心身ともに休まる気がします。

　どの町でも役所の人力車が使えるよう、知事が特別な書類を書いてくれました。また、わたしが乗るまで船出を遅らせるようにとも指示してあります。これには本当に感謝しています。

　まえに七飯(ななえ)の村を通り過ぎたとき、振り返って函館半島の荘厳な景色を見ました。紺碧の海に浮かぶ島のようでした。もっと高い山からは、夕焼けのピンク色の光を浴びる火山のすばらしい光景を眺めました。ここの景観は本州のものとはずいぶん違っていて、見ていると新しい命を与えられる気がするのです。

Ginsainoma, Yezo
August 17

I am in the wild once again! I am sitting outside a house built over a lake. Coming down the nearest hill are men who have just killed a bear with spears. I am completely alone, which is so refreshing. Leaving Ito for a day in Hakodate, I've ridden here alone. With some Japanese words, I got a comfortable room for the night and a meal of rice, eggs, and beans. I am not off the "**beaten track**" yet, but I am excited to journey into **the land of the Aino, Japan's aborigines**. The wild, northern countryside is beautiful, and I feel well rested.

The governor wrote me a special letter that will allow me to use the government's *kuruma* in each town. It also instructs any boat to delay its departure until I am on it. I am very grateful for this.

Once we traveled past the village of Nanai, I looked back to see a glorious view of Hakodate Head. It almost looked like an island in the deep blue sea. From a higher hill, I got a wonderful view of the volcano in the pink light of sunset. The landscape here is very different from the mainland, and it gives me new life to see it.

噴火湾、森にて、月曜日——伊藤は上機嫌です。わたしと同じように北海道の自由な雰囲気を楽しんでいます。それに、知事からもらった書類が誇らしいのでしょう。伊藤は宿屋に泊まるたびに、その書類を見せびらかしています。森は、噴火湾の南端近くにある、大きくて古ぼけたような村です。**この北の地では、季節はすでに変わりはじめています。**山肌に黄色や赤い場所が点々とあり、秋の到来を知らせています。

蝦夷、勇払(ゆうふつ)にて——すばらしい好天の日に、室蘭(むろらん)行きの船に乗りました。水は青く、海の泡は白く、火山の赤い灰が日差しを浴びて輝いています。室蘭の背後に山があり、その向こうの海岸沿いに最初のアイヌの村があるのです。

次に幌別(ほろべつ)という、アイヌと日本人が混ざって住んでいる海辺の町へ向かいました。混住の村では、アイヌは日本人からかなり離れて暮らしています。幌別には47軒のアイヌの家と、18軒の日本人の家があります。アイヌの家のことは、もっとよくわかってからお伝えすることにします。今のところは、日本人の家というより、**ポリネシア人の家のようだ**ということだけ言っておきましょう。木の枠に葦(あし)をしっかりと結びつけて作っているからです。海辺に住むアイヌはみんな漁をしますが、この季節には男たちが森で鹿を狩ります。

幌別のアイヌの倉
Aino Store-House at Horobets

Mori, Volcano Bay, Monday—Ito is in a good mood. Like me, he enjoys the freedom of the Hokkaido, and he is proud of our letter from the governor. He shows it off at every *yadoya* we stop at. Mori is a large, worn-down looking village near the southern point of Volcano Bay. **Here, in the north, the season is already changing**. There are a few spots of yellow and red on the hillside, signaling that autumn is coming.

Yubets, Yezo—We took a boat to Mororan on a splendid day. The water was blue, the sea foam was white, and the red ash of the volcano glowed in the sun. There is a hill that lies behind Mororan, and beyond this is the first Aino village along this coast.

We traveled next to Horobets, an Aino-Japanese mixed village on the beach. In mixed villages, the Aino live at a respectful distance from the Japanese. At Horobets, there are forty-seven Aino houses and eighteen Japanese houses. I will describe Aino houses later when I understand them better. But for now, I'll say that they **look like Polynesian houses** more than Japanese, because they are made of reeds carefully tied onto a wooden frame. Coastal Ainos all fish, but during this season the men hunt deer in the forests.

幌別からは、人力車を引くのに3人のアイヌを雇いました——ふたりの少年と、ひとりの大人の男です。ふたりの少年たちは、唇の厚い大きな口をしていました。エスキモー人によく似ています。やわらかくて長い髪が顔の両側にたれていました。大人の男は純粋なアイヌではありません。とても美しい顔立ちに、悲しげで知的な目をしていました。

　3人は不平も言わずに人力車を引き、わたしが快適に乗れるようにとても気遣ってくれました。いくつかの村を過ぎましたが、そこには、ひどい臭いのする小屋がありました——これは魚油を作る小屋だとわかりました。川まで来ると、その美しいアイヌがわたしに、肩に乗るよう合図しました。そして肩まである川の水のなかを歩いて渡って、わたしを運んでくれたのです。

　暗くなった頃、海のそばの混住の村、白老に着きました。伊藤が、とてもきれいで新しい宿屋を見つけ、そこで新鮮な鮭を使ったおいしい夕食を食べました。

　佐瑠太（さるふと）——この地方での朝一番の音は、**何百頭もの馬が、アイヌたちに追われて囲いのほうへ殺到する音**です。馬たちは荒々しく山を駆けめぐっていますが、アイヌたちが大きな群れを毎日集めて、その日の必要に応じて囲いに入れるのです。

　今朝、3人のアイヌとともに、野生の花に囲まれた道を出発しました。歩いていると、4人のきれいなアイヌの女たちに出会いました。いろいろ話したり笑ったりしたあと、女たちは男たちと一緒に人力車を引きはじめ、笑いながら

From Horobets, we hired three Aino to pull our *kuruma*—two youths and one man. The two boys had thick lips and wide mouths. They looked rather like Eskimos. Their soft, long hair fell down each side of their faces. The adult man was not a pure Aino. He was beautiful and had sad, intelligent eyes.

They pulled my *kuruma* without complaint and were very concerned about my comfort. We passed a few villages, where a bad smell came from some sheds—I found out these are used for making fish oil. When we came to a river, the beautiful Aino signaled for me to climb onto his shoulders. He carried me across as he walked through the river up to his shoulders.

At dark, we arrived at Shiraoi, a Japanese-Aino mixed village near the sea. Ito found a very pretty, new *yadoya*, and we had a delicious dinner of fresh salmon.

Sarufuto—The first sound in the morning in this region is **the stampede of a hundred horses being corralled by the Aino**. Horses run quite wild in the hills, and the Ainos gather a large herd every day and drive them into a corral for the day's needs.

This morning we set out with three Ainos along a road surrounded by wild flowers. As we walked, we met four pretty Aino women. After much talking and laughing, the women joined the men and they all

全速力で半マイルも走ったのです。文明の固定観念から離れて自然のなかにいるのは、なんて楽しいのでしょう！ つぎに、馬に乗った4人の日本人に出会うと、アイヌたちは彼らと競争しました。こうして走ってばかりいたので、正午には苫小牧に着いたのです！

　そこから、道と電話線は内陸のほうへ曲がって、札幌へ向かいます。わたしたちは馬に乗って海沿いに、草花に覆われた起伏のゆるやかな砂原を8マイル進みました。やがて勇払に着きましたが、ここは見たことがないほど寂しいところでした。日本人の家が4、5軒、アイヌの小屋が4つ、魚油を作る小屋が少し、そして細長くて灰色の漁業基地があるだけです。漁の季節になると、その建物の30から40の部屋に、最高300人の男たちが寝泊まりします。でも今は空っぽで、管理人とふたりの孤児の少年がいるだけです。

アイヌの小屋
Aino Lodges

pulled my *kuruma*, running at top speed and laughing for half a mile. How nice it is to be in nature and away from the stereotypes of civilization! Next, we met four Japanese on horseback, and the Aino raced them. With all this running, I reached Tomakomai at noon!

From there, the roads and telegraph wires turn inland, towards Satsuporo. We rode horses for eight miles along the sea across rolling, sandy plains covered with flowers and grass. Then, we arrived in Yubets, the most lonely-looking place I've ever seen. It consisted of just four or five Japanese houses, four Aino huts, some fish-oil sheds, and a long, grey fishing station. During the fishing season, the building's thirty or forty rooms accommodate up to three hundred men. But now, the building is empty except for the caretaker and two orphan boys.

漁業基地の外には、長く延びた灰色の浜と、暗灰色の海があるだけです。浜には2艘の丸木舟がありました。丸木舟のそばに2、3人のアイヌが見えました——動物の毛皮を着て、とても威厳があります。また、狼のような犬を数匹連れていました。それにしても、海の音、海鳥の鳴き声、そして風の音は、まるで音楽のように聞こえます。世界のどこにいても、自然はつねに調和を生み出すのです。

　佐瑠太のつづき——ここの田舎は美しく、再び太陽が輝いています。今日はいい馬に乗って、花の咲く美しい草原を17マイル進みました。今は、日本人の家が63軒ある村にいます。**入植による開拓地**で、人口のほとんどが仙台からの移民です。アイヌは悪意のないやさしい人々ですが、**日本人はアイヌを見下しています**。

　平取（びらとり）という、アイヌの村へ行って泊まる予定です。わたしは伊藤に、アイヌに敬意をもって接してほしいと頼みましたが、彼は、「アイヌはただの犬で、人間じゃありませんよ！」と答えるのです。

Outside the fishing station, there was only a long, grey beach and dark grey ocean. On the beach were a couple of wooden canoes. I saw two or three Ainos near the canoes—they were grand, dressed in animal skins. They had several dogs that looked like wolves. But the sound of the sea, the call of the sea birds, and the whistling of the wind sounded like music. Nature always produces harmony, no matter where in the world you are.

Sarufuto, continued—The countryside here is beautiful, and the sun is shining again. I rode seventeen miles today on a good horse over beautiful, flowery grasslands. I am now in a village of sixty-three Japanese houses. **It is a colonization settlement**, and the population is mostly from Sendai. **The Japanese look down on the Aino**, although the Aino are a harmless, gentle people.

We will travel to Biratori, the Aino village where I will stay. I told Ito that I want him to treat the Aino with respect, but his response is "They're just dogs, not men!"

平取、
アイヌの小屋にて
8月23日

　この3日間、アイヌの小屋で、アイヌの家族とともに過ごしています。この旅で一番おもしろい経験となっています。馬に乗ったアイヌのガイドが、森を抜けてこの平取まで連れてきてくれました。わたしたちは、宿泊中の食べ物と調理器具を持っていかなければなりませんでした。

　平取は、この地域でもっとも大きなアイヌの村です。森や山、川がそばにあって美しいですが、寂しいところです。はじめは首長のベンリの家に寄りました。ベンリは留守でしたが、甥のシノンディとほかの男たちが、このうえなく丁重に迎えてくれました。**そして手を内側に振ってから、あごひげをなでるという、彼らの風習で挨拶をしました。**

アイヌの首長
An Aino Patriarch

たいへん礼儀正しくて、馬から荷物をおろすのを手伝い、すぐに食べ物を出してくれました。そのうえ、わたしのベッドのそばに一番いいむしろを敷くのです。彼らによると、ベンリはわたしに、泊まりたいだけ泊まってほしい、また、暮らし方や習慣が違うことを許し

Aino Hut, Biratori August 23

アイヌの小屋
Aino Houses

For the past three days, I have been living in an Aino hut with an Aino family. It has been the most interesting part of my journey. An Aino guide on a horse brought us here, through the forest, to Biratori. We had to bring all of our own food and cooking utensils for our stay.

Biratori is the largest Aino village in this region. It is beautifully located among forests, mountains, and a river, but it is a lonely place. We first stopped at the house of Benri, the chief. Benri was away, but Shinondi, his nephew, and several other men received us with the greatest respect. **They greeted us by waving their hands inward and stroking their beards, which is their custom.** They were extremely polite, helping us unload our horses and offering food immediately. They placed their best mats by my bed. They told me that Benri welcomed me to stay as long as I wanted and asked me to excuse them for having different ways and customs than my own.

てほしいと言っていたそうです。

　夕方になると、18人くらいの人がベンリの家に、「歓迎の意を表しに」やってきました。何人かは堂々とした老人で、たっぷりした灰色のあごひげを生やしていました。ここでは、**年配者はたいへん尊敬されます**。わたしはみんなに煙草を回しながら、自分は日が沈む方向の、はるか遠くの海に浮かぶ地からやってきたこと、また、アイヌのことについて自国の人に話せるよう、いろいろな質問するためにやってきたことを伝えました。

　シノンディと村のほかの4人は日本語が話せます。わたしたちはアイヌの男たちと何時間も話しました。わたしの質問と彼らの答えは、英語から日本語、そしてアイヌ語へと通訳され、それからまた逆に通訳されるのです。ただ、まず話すまえに、**アイヌの習慣をわたしに話したことを日本政府に言わないでほしいと頼まれました**。でないと、面倒なことになるというのです！ アイヌたちはたいへん礼儀正しくて、伊藤でさえ、想像していたよりいい人たちだと言っています。

　アイヌたちは、キビの粉や根菜、さや豆、海草、干し魚、鹿肉を煮込んだものを食べると、酒を取り出しました。漆塗りの椀に注ぎ、みごとに彫刻された「捧酒箸（イクパスイ）」という箸を、椀に上に渡して置きました。この箸は、火と神々に酒を捧げるために使われるのです。捧げ物が終わると、みんなで酒を飲みはじめました。

　翌日の朝食後、シノンディを連れて、ほかの村人たちの家を訪れました。みんな心からの敬意をもって挨拶してくれましたが、家に入れないようにとシノンディに頼む人

That evening, about eighteen men came to Benri's house to "bid me welcome." Several were grand-looking old men with full, grey beards. **Age is greatly respected here**. Handing around some tobacco, I told them that I came from a land in the sea, very far away, where they saw the sun go down, and that I had come to ask them many questions, so that I could tell my own people about them.

Shinondi and four others in the village speak Japanese. We spoke with the Aino men for many hours. My questions and their answers went from English to Japanese to Aino, and back again. But before they told me anything, **they begged me not to tell the Japanese Government that they shared their customs with me**, or they may get into trouble! They are an extremely polite people, and even Ito says they are better than he expected.

After they ate a stew of ground millet, roots, green beans, seaweed, dried fish, and venison, they brought out the *sake*. They poured it into lacquered bowls and lay a finely carved "*sake* stick" across the bowl. These sticks are used to make *sake* offerings to the fire and to the gods. After these offerings were made, they all drank.

After breakfast the next day, Shinondi took me to visit the homes of some other villagers. They all greeted me with profound respect, but some asked

もいました。自分たちの貧しさを、わたしに見られたくなかったからです。

どの家にも低い棚があって、すばらしい置物がいくつかありましたが、それを除けば、家はがらんとしていました。毎年動物の毛皮を売っているので、そのお金でいいものをたくさん買って家に置けるでしょうに、余分なものは欲しくも必要でもないらしいのです。

アイヌは流浪の民ではありません。先祖が住んでいた土地に、ずっととどまっています。ただ、農作はかなり下手なようです。キビ、カボチャ、玉ねぎ、ジャガイモといった作物の畑には、雑草がびっしり生えています。狩猟と漁業が男たちの主な仕事です。家のなかでの仕事は、木を彫って品物を作ることです——たとえば、捧酒箸、煙草入れ、ナイフの鞘などです。木彫をしていないときは、楽しそうにただ煙草を吸ったり、食べたり、眠ったりしています。

アイヌの家族
Ainos at Home

Shinondi not to take me into their houses because they did not want me to see how poor they are.

All the houses have a low shelf with a few fine items on it, but aside from this, their houses are bare. The animal skins they sell every year are worth enough to surround them with nice things, but they do not seem to want or need extra things.

The Aino are not nomads. They stay on the same land where their fathers lived. But they seem to be terrible farmers. Weeds crowd their crops of millet, pumpkins, onions, and potatoes. Hunting and fishing are the main activities of the men. Their indoor activities are to carve things out of wood—*sake* sticks, tobacco boxes, and knife sheaths, for example. When they are not doing this, they seem happy to simply smoke, eat, and sleep.

ところが、女たちはいつも忙しくしています。薪を割ったり、キビをひいたり、畑仕事をしたり、裁縫をしたり、布を織ったり、樹皮を裂いたりしています。樹皮を裂くのは、**それで衣服を作るからです。**アイヌの樹皮布は丈夫な素材なので、日本人の下層階級でも着る人がいます。

機織りの〜ラ
Weaver's Shuttle

　昨日は男たちが狩猟に出かけたので、わたしと、ベンリの正妻と母親を含む約7人の女だけが残りました。女たちのなかには、日本語を話せる人もいるのがわかりました。彼女たちの暮らしについていくつか質問したあと、ヨーロッパの女たちの暮らしについて訊かれました。**みんなしだいに打ち解けて、**いきいきと話したり、笑ったりしていました。

　午後になると、立派なアイヌの若者が、漁をしていた浜辺からやってきました。これはベンリの養子で、名前はピピチャリといいます。木の根っこで足を切ったので、わたしに見てほしいと言いました。わたしが傷を洗おうとすると、自分の足はとても汚いのに、あなたの手は「白すぎる」から触らないでほしい、と言います。傷を包帯で巻いてあげると、彼は深くお辞儀をして、わたしの手にキスをしたのです！

　ピピチャリはわたしの持ち物にとても興味を示しました。わたしのはさみを見、ブーツに触り、字を書くのをじっと見つめていました。自分は酒を飲まないから、ほかの人が近寄らないのだと言います。酒を飲まないことで

アイヌの臼と杵
Aino Millet-Mille and Pestle

The women, however, are always busy. They chop wood, grind millet, farm, sew, weave, and split bark, **because this is what they make their clothes out of**. The Aino bark cloth is an indestructible material that some of the lower classes of Japanese also wear.

Yesterday, the men went away to hunt and I was left alone with about seven women, including Benri's first wife and his mother. Some of the women, we discovered, spoke Japanese. After I asked them some questions about their life, they asked me about the life of European women. **They began to open up**, talking and laughing in a lively way.

In the afternoon, a fine young Aino came up from the coast where he had been fishing. This was Benri's adopted son, named Pipichari. He had cut his foot on a root and asked me to look at it. When I tried to wash the wound, he said he did not want me to touch it, because his foot was too dirty and my hands were "too white." When I finished dressing his wound, he bowed low and kissed my hand!

Pipichari was very curious about my things. He looked at my scissors, touched my boots, and watched me as I wrote. He says he does not drink *sake*, and the others stay away from him because they think the

神々が彼に怒っていると、人々は思っているからです。

　昨夜、「息が苦しい」と訴えている女がいると言うので、見にいきました。女はむしろの上に横になり、気管支炎にかかって弱っていました。わたしは何度かようすを見にいきました。もう死ぬのではないかと不安になったときもありましたが、クロロダインと牛肉スープ、そして注意深く看病することで治すことができました。人々は大喜びして、わたしをアイヌたちの神社へ招いてくれました。

　翌日、アイヌたちはわたしを険しい崖の上へ連れていきました。彼らの神社の前に立っていることは**とても光栄で、謙虚な気持ちにさせられました**。ほかの外国人は誰も来たことがないのです。神社は、崖の端に立つ簡素な木造の建物でした。アイヌたちは引き戸を開けて、全員お辞儀をしました。奥に棚があり、その上に真鍮の義経像や、ふたつのろうそく立て、金属製の御幣、中国船の絵が置かれています。アイヌたちは3回鐘を鳴らして、3回お辞儀をし、義経像に6回酒を捧げました。それから、わたしにも神を拝むようにと言いましたが、**自分の宗教があるからそれはできないと答えました**。彼らはとても礼儀正しいので、それ以上押しつけるようなことはしませんでした。

gods are angry with him for not drinking.

Last night, I went to see a woman who the Ainos said was "having trouble breathing." I found her lying on a mat, weak and struggling with bronchitis. I visited several times. At one point I was afraid the woman was going to die, but I was able to make her better with chlorodyne, beef tea, and close monitoring. The people were so overjoyed that they invited me to see their shrine.

The next day, they took me up a steep cliff. **I felt honored and humble** to be standing before their shrine, where no other foreigner had been. The shrine is a simple, wooden structure standing at the edge of a cliff. When they opened the sliding doors, they all bowed. There was a shelf at the back holding a brass figure of Yoshitsune, two candlesticks, some metal *gohei*, and a picture of a Chinese boat. They rang the bell three times, bowed three times, and made six offerings of *sake* to the figure of Yoshitsune. They asked me to worship their god but **I told them I could not, due to my own religion**. They were too polite to press any further.

平取にて

8月24日

　アイヌについてもっとお話ししましょう。彼らはまさに未開人です——字が書けず、数字も千以上は数えられません——それでも、**ほれぼれするほど魅力的な民族です**。アイヌは、太陽、月、火、水を崇め、自分たちは犬の子孫だと信じています。見かけは獰猛そうですが、その笑顔は、ほかでは見たことがないほど好ましいものです。

　男たちは胸が広く、短い手足をしています。村にいる30人の男たちの身長を計ると、5フィート4インチから5フィート6インチでした。顔つきはアジア人よりヨーロッパ人に似ています。髪は多くて黒く、ほぼ肩につくまで伸ばし、真ん中で分けています。

　アイヌの女たちは、身長が5フィートを超えることはめったにありませんが、身体つきは美しく、小さな手足に、ふくよかな胸、そしてきれいな歯並びをしています。髪型は男たちと同様です。女たちはみな、口のまわり

アイヌの男たち
Two Aino male

Biratori, Yezo
August 24

Let me describe the Aino further. They are complete savages—they have no writing or numbers over a thousand—**yet they are attractive and fascinating**. They worship the sun, moon, fire, and water, and they believe they are descended from a dog. They are ferocious looking, but their smiles are some of the sweetest I've ever seen.

The men have broad chests and short limbs. I have measured the height of thirty men in the village, and they range between 5 feet 4 inches to 5 feet 6 inches. Their features are more European than Asian. Their hair is thick and black. They wear it long, almost touching their shoulders, and parted in the middle.

Aino women are rarely more than five feet tall, but they are beautifully formed, with small hands and feet, well-developed busts, and straight teeth. They wear their hair like the men. All the women are tattooed around the mouth, across

婦人の手の入れ墨
Tattooed Female Hand

や、指の付け根、手の甲、手首から肘にかけて入れ墨を入れています。入れ墨は5歳から入れはじめます。ひとりの女が娘に初めての入れ墨を入れているのを、わたしは見ました。大きなナイフを手に取り、口のすぐ近くを水平に小さく切ると、その傷口に黒いすすをすり込むのです。入れ墨は、少女が結婚するまで毎年増やされます。男たちによれば、これは古くからある風習で、入れ墨のない女は結婚できないそうです。

子どもたちは4歳か5歳になるまで名前がなく、そのときが来ると父親が名前を選びます。赤ん坊のときから、従順でよく手伝うようにしつけられます。7歳か8歳になるまで衣服を身につけません。

アイヌの衣服はとても丈夫で良質です。冬には動物の毛皮のコートを着て、夏には樹皮で作った着物を着ます。樹皮の布で作るぴっちりした脚絆(きゃはん)は男も女もはきますが、靴は冬に狩猟に行く男しかはきません。また、アイヌの女は人前ではけっして服を着替えたり脱いだりしません。

アイヌが祝日に着る晴れ着は非常に美しく、幾何学模様で飾られています。模様は青い布に赤と白の糸で縁どりをして作ります。なかには、作るのに半年かかるものもあるそうです。女たちは銀や白目(しろめ)【訳注:スズを主成分とする合金】の輪のイヤリングと銀のネックレス、そして真鍮のブレスレットを少し身につけます。

アイヌの家の建築様式は、**日本風というよりヨーロッパ**

the knuckles, on the back of the hand, and on the arms up to the elbows. The tattooing begins at age five. I watched a woman tattoo her daughter for the first time. She took a large knife and cut little horizontal lines very close to the mouth, then rubbed some black soot into the cuts. The tattoo is widened every year until the girl is married. The men say it is an old custom and that no woman can marry without it.

Children are not named until they are four or five years old, when the father chooses the name. They are expected to be obedient and helpful from the time they are babies. They wear no clothing until they are seven or eight years old.

Aino clothing is very durable and good. In the winter they wear coats made of animal skins, and in the summer they wear *kimonos* made of bark. Tight leggings made of bark cloth is worn by both men and women, but shoes are not worn except by men going hunting in the winter. An Aino woman will not change or take her clothes off in front of anyone, ever.

The special clothes that Ainos wear for holidays are very beautiful, decorated with geometric patterns. The patterns are made from blue cloth braided with red and white thread. Some take half a year to make. The women wear silver or pewter hoop earrings, silver necklaces, and a few brass bracelets.

The architecture of the Aino house is **more**

風です。戸口や窓があり、寝床も高くしてあるのです。どの家にも2部屋あります。家に入ると窓のない小さな部屋があり、すり鉢や、すりこぎ、狩猟道具など、家族で使う道具が置かれています。それから戸口を通って大きな部屋へ入ります。屋根はとても高くて、傾斜が急です。

　家の骨組は4本の柱で、これが4本の梁を支えています。壁は葦を2層に重ねて作られています。屋根の端のほうに、煙を出すための大きな三角形の穴があります。戸口の左手に高さ18インチの木製の台があり、むしろで覆われています。これが寝床です。真ん中にあるのは囲炉裏で、大きな鍋がその上にぶらさがっています。**どの家にも「家の守り神」があります。**丸まった白い削りくずを先端からぶらさげた白い細枝が、たいてい入口の左手の壁に刺してあるのです。また、「偉大なる神」は高さ2フィートくらいの白い棒で、これにも渦巻状の白い削りくずがついています。

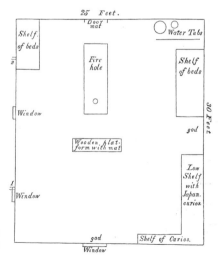

アイヌの家屋の平面図
Plan of an Aino House

European than that of the Japanese because they have doors and windows, and raised beds. Each house is made of two rooms. You enter through a small room with no windows where some of the family's tools, such as the mortar and pestle and hunting gear, are kept. Then you walk through a door into the larger room. The roof is very high and steep.

The frame of the house is four posts, which support four cross-beams. The walls are made of two layers of reeds. There is a large triangle-shaped opening on the far side of the roof for smoke to exit. To the left of the door is a wooden platform about 18-inches high, covered with a mat. This is the sleeping place. In the center is a fireplace with a large cooking pot hanging over it. **There are "household gods" in every house.**

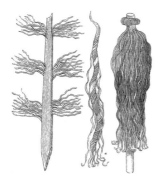

アイヌの神像
Aino Gods

これは壁のそばに置かれ、その上に小さな棚があって、珍しい日本の工芸品が載っています。そのうちのいくつかは、とても貴重な骨董品で、金の漆塗りに真珠の象眼細工が施されています。こういう品物はたぶん、アイヌの男たちが将軍へ貢ぎ物を届けに行ったとき、力のある大名から贈られたものなのでしょう。

アイヌはふだん、キビを煮込んだものや、魚、海草、なめくじ、山菜、野イチゴ、木や草の根、鹿や熊の肉を食べます。箸を使って食べ、1日2回しか食事しません。男たちは、秋、冬、春に狩猟をします。毒矢で狩るのですが、最近それを政府から禁止されたそうです。

アイヌの宗教ほど**漠然としてまとまりのないもの**は、ほかにないでしょう。崖の上の神社以外、寺も、僧侶も、礼拝もありません。原始的な自然崇拝を行ないながら、義経も崇めています。彼はずっと昔にアイヌを助けたと信じられているのです。再びアイヌを助けにくると信じている人もいます。このほかには、彼らの信仰には力強い物語も理由もありません。**単純に自分たちよりも強い力があると信じ、また、酒によって邪悪なものを遠ざけることができる**と信じているのです。**アイヌの唯一の礼拝は、「神のために飲むこと」**です。そして狩猟や漁の季節の終わりには、ふたつの神聖な言葉を唱えます。

White wands, with curly white shavings hanging from the top, are usually stuck in the walls to the left of the entrance. The "great god" is a white post about two feet high that also has white spiral shavings. This is placed near a wall, and above it is a little shelf containing Japanese curios and works of art. Some of them are very valuable antiques with gold lacquer and pearl inlay. These items were probably given to Aino men by powerful *daimyo* when they went to pay tribute to the Shogun.

The Aino usually eat millet stew, as well as fish, seaweed, slugs, wild vegetables, wild berries, roots, venison, and bear. They eat with chopsticks and only eat twice a day. The men hunt in the autumn, winter, and spring. They hunt with poison arrows, which was recently been banned by the government.

There cannot be anything more **vague and lacking cohesion** than Aino religion. Except for the shrine on the cliff, they have no temples, priests, or form of worshipping. They practice a primitive nature worship, and they also revere Yoshitsune, who they believe helped the Aino a long time ago. Some believe he will come to help them again. Other than this, there is no strong narrative or reason for any of their beliefs. **They simply believe there are powers stronger than them**, and they can keep evil away with *sake*. **Their only form of worship is to "drink to the gods."** They chant two religious sayings at the end of hunting

「われらに食べ物を与えてくれる海に、われらを守ってくれる森に、心から感謝します。あなたたちは同じ子を養うふたりの母親です。われらがひとりの母のもとを去って、もうひとりの母のもとへ行っても、どうか怒らないでください」

「アイヌはつねに森と海を誇りに思うでしょう」

アイヌの唯一の祭りは熊祭りです。祭りでは、熊をわなで捕えて、殺し、皮をはぎ、そして食べるのです。アイヌの村には、地面から高さ2、3フィートの大きな木製の檻があります。この檻は、祭り用の若い熊を入れるために作られたものです。男たちが野生の子熊を捕えて首長の家に連れてくると、女たちが世話をしたり、子どもたちが一緒に遊んだりします。やがて大きくなって暴れるようになると檻に入れ、熊祭りが行なわれる日まで、エサを与えて世話をします。この祭りのしきたりには、山のアイヌと海岸のアイヌとでかなり違いがあります。とはいえ、どこでも人々は祭りに集まって宴会を開き、酒を飲んで踊るのです。

男たちが叫んだり怒鳴ったりして熊を興奮させ、熊が怒りだすと、首長が熊を矢で射ます。こうして逆上させた熊を檻から出すのです。すると、アイヌたちが武器を持って走り寄り、誰もが熊に傷を負わせようとします。そうすることで幸運が得られるからです。熊が疲れて倒れたら、すぐに頭を切り落とし、武器は熊に捧げられます。そのあと、みんなで肉を食べ、熊の頭は柱の上に置かれて崇めら

and fishing seasons:

"To the sea which feeds us, to the forest which protects us, we present our grateful thanks. You are two mothers that nourish the same child; do not be angry if we leave one to go to the other.

"The Ainos will always be the pride of the forest and of the sea."

Their one festival is the Bear Festival, in which they trap, kill, skin, and eat a bear. In Aino villages, there is a large cage made of wood, raised two or three feet from the ground. The cage is made to contain a young bear for the festival. The men catch a bear cub in the wild and bring it to the home of the chief, where a woman nurses the bear and the children play with it. When it grows too big and rough it is placed in the cage. It is fed and cared for until the Festival of the Bear is celebrated. The customs of this festival vary among the mountain and coast Ainos. But everywhere, the people gather for the festival, have a feast, drink *sake*, and dance.

The men excite the bear by yelling and shouting, and when the bear becomes angry, the chief shoots him with an arrow. This maddens the bear, and it is let out of the cage. This is when the Ainos run at it with weapons, each one hoping to inflict a wound, as this brings good luck. As soon as the bear falls down exhausted, his head is cut off, and the weapons are

れます。(のちに、噴火湾の有珠で老人から聞いたのですが、その地の祭りでは熊を別の方法で殺すそうです。檻から出すとき、ふたりの男が熊の耳をつかみ、ほかの男たちが長い棒を熊の首の後ろに当てます。それから大勢のアイヌたちが棒の上に積み重なるように乗るので、やがて熊の首の骨が折れてしまいます。そのとき、男たちはこう叫ぶのです。「熊よ、おまえを殺すぞ！　すぐにアイヌになって戻ってこい」)

　アイヌの男に対する最高のほめ言葉は、熊にたとえることです。ですから、シノンディは首長のベンリのことを「熊のように強い」と言います。

offered to it. Afterwards all the people eat the meat, and the bear's head is put on a pole and worshipped. [Afterwards at Usu, on Volcano Bay, the old men told me that at their festival they kill the bear in a different way. When they let it loose from the cage, two men grab it by the ears, and the others lay a long pole across the back of its neck. A number of Ainos pile on top of pole until the neck is broken. The men then shout, "We kill you, O bear! Come back soon as an Aino."]

The highest compliment one can pay to a man is to compare him to a bear. Thus Shinondi says of Benri, the chief, "He is as strong as a bear."

蝦夷、佐瑠太にて
8月27日

　昨日、アイヌを後にしたのはとても残念でした。とはいえ、服のまま眠ったり、お風呂に入れないのにうんざりしていたのは本当だと認めねばなりません。ベンリの2人の妻が朝からキビをひいて粉にし、キビ餅を作ってくれました。また村を去るまえに、村人が別れの挨拶に出てきて、熊の皮などの贈り物をくれました。

　門別(もんべつ)へ向かうと、**そこは27軒の家がばらばらに点在する、哀れなようすの村でした。**アイヌの家と、日本人の家があります。今は魚や海草をとったり、魚油を作ったりする季節なので、いつもより多くの漁師が村にいます。でも海が荒れて舟を出せないので、男たちはみんな1日じゅう酒を飲んでいます。アイヌ人も日本人もひどいありさまで、よろめいたり、倒れたり、すっかり酔っぱらって床で眠ったりしています。その姿を見ていると悲しくなりました。

　月曜日——海がひどく荒れて、馬が門別から先へわたしを運べないので、もう1日ここで足止めになっています。昨日、ピピチャリがわたしに会いにきて、丁寧に彫った木製のナイフの鞘をくれました。外は嵐だったので、ピピチャリは午後のほとんどをわたしの部屋の隅で寝ころがって過ごし、わたしがメモできるようアイヌの言葉を教えてくれました。

Sarufuto, Yezo
August 27

I was sad to leave the Ainos yesterday, although I must admit that I was tired of sleeping in my clothes and not bathing. Benri's two wives spent the morning grinding millet and making them into cakes. Before I left, the villagers came to say goodbye and brought me gifts, including a bear skin.

We traveled to Mombets, **a wretched cluster of twenty-seven homes falling apart**. Some were Aino, some Japanese. It is fishing, seaweed, and fish-oil season now, so there are more fishermen than usual at the village. But because the seas were so rough and the boats could not go out, all the men had spent the day drinking. Both the Aino and Japanese were sorry sights, stumbling, falling, and sleeping on the ground completely drunk. It made me sad to see it.

Monday—Because the seas are so rough and the horse cannot carry me past Mombets, I am stuck here for another day. Pipichari came to visit me yesterday, bringing a wooden knife sheath that he had carefully carved. It was storming outside, so he spent most of the afternoon lying in a corner of my room, giving me more Aino words to write down.

蝦夷、噴火湾、旧室蘭にて
9月2日

　今は白老に戻っていますが、わたしはここがとても気に入っています。まわりはおもしろい火山の風景で、昨日は1日じゅう、アイヌのガイドと一緒に見てまわりました。近くの山の尾根が、じつは円錐形の石灰華【編注：炭酸カルシウムの塊状沈殿物】が連なったものではないかと思い、調べたくてしかたなかったのです。もの静かで親切な信頼のおけるアイヌのガイドと一緒に、伊藤を置いて出かけ、すばらしい1日を過ごしました。観察して学ぶことが山ほどありました。密林のなかを、へとへとになりながら歩いたあと、ひとつの山の山腹に着きました。山肌の裂け目から、蒸気や煙が出ています。なかに腕を入れてみると、とても熱いので、すぐに引っ込めなければなりませんでした。さらに進むと温泉がありましたが、こちらは持ってきた温度計が壊れるほどの熱さです！　そして尾根は、うれしいことに、たしかに石灰華だとわかりました。ガイドもわたしも馬から落とされたり、泥水のなかに落ちたり、密林で引っかき傷や切り傷を負ったりと、たしかにくたびれる行程でしたが、**わたしには何よりも楽しい探検だったのです！**

　つづき――今朝、ふたりの親切な未開人が引く人力車で、白老を出発しました。先日の暴風雨で道の多くが洗い流されていたので、人力車から降りて、かなりの道を歩かなけ

Old Mororan, Volcano Bay, Yezo
September 2

I am now back in Shiraoi. I like it here very much. There are interesting volcanic landscapes all around, which I spent all day yesterday exploring with an Aino guide. I was curious to find out if a nearby mountain ridge were actually a series of volcanic tufa cones. My silent, kind, and trustworthy Aino guide and I set off without Ito and had a splendid day. There was a great deal to learn and see. After an exhausting trek through jungle, we reached the side of one of the mountains. There was steam and smoke coming out of a crack in the mountain wall. When I put my arm in, I had to pull it out quickly because it was so hot. Further on, we came to a spring hot enough to burst one of my thermometers! The ridge, I was delighted to find, was indeed made of tufa cones. Although it was an exhausting journey in which both my guide and I got kicked off our horses, fell into mud, and got scratched and cut by the jungle, **I enjoyed that exploration more than anything!**

Continued—This morning I left Shiraoi in a *kuruma* pulled by two kind savages. With the recent rainstorms, many of the roads were washed out and

ればなりませんでした。でも人力車に戻るたびに、アイヌたちは空気枕を直し、毛布をひざにかけてくれました。**わたしたちみんなが、「やさしさ」という共通の言葉を持っているのはすばらしいことです。**そして世界じゅうどこでも、笑顔の持つ意味は同じなのです。

　幌別で、旧室蘭へ向かうために馬を雇いました。その馬は、これまで日本で見たことがないほど強くてきれいな馬でした。でも旅のあいだじゅう雨が降っていたので、旧室蘭に着いたころには、すっかりぬれてしまいました。もう真夜中ですが、まだ起きたまま、ベッドと服を囲炉裏の火で乾かしているのです。

I had to get out of the *kuruma* and walk much of the way. But each time I got back into the *kuruma*, the Ainos fixed my air-pillow and put a blanket over me. **It is wonderful we all have one language in common: kindness**. A smile anywhere in the world means the same thing.

At Horobets I hired a horse to bring me to Old Mororan. It was the strongest, prettiest horse I have seen in Japan so far, but it rained during our whole journey and I arrived in Old Mororan completely soaked. Now it's midnight, but I'm still awake trying to dry my bed and clothes by the fire.

函館にて
9月12日

　礼文華(れぶんげ)はとても孤立したところで、それゆえに、たいへん興味深いところです。日本人の宿の主人——ここでの唯一の日本人——は、アイヌたちにとても親切です。彼はアイヌたちみんなに、わたしに会いに来てもいいと言いました。そこで、アイヌたちは子どもたちを連れてやってくると、高く抱きあげてわたしに見せてくれました。

　礼文華のアイヌは、東のほうのアイヌとはかなり違います。肌はとても黒く、額は低くて、目がくぼみ、背はもっと低くて、毛もさらに濃いのです。ここのアイヌは、眉の上の毛を2インチほど剃っています。

　彼らの村から、17マイルという最長の旅程に出発しました。**この道は本当に人けがないので、4日間の旅のあいだ、道でひとりも人に出会いませんでした。**礼文華谷は深い森と岩地に覆われています。わたしたちは狭い尾根を伝って進み続け、竹林を抜け、岩だらけの峡谷を過ぎました。**ときどき道が消えるので、ガイドは絶対に必要でした。**それにしても、これほど雄大な森は見たことがありません。

　長万部(おしゃまんべ)へ着くころまでに、背中がとても痛くなったので、1日泊まって休まなければなりませんでした。長万部は悲

Hakodate
September 12

Lebunge is extremely isolated, making it very interesting. The Japanese house-master—who was the only Japanese there—was very kind to the Ainos. He told them they could all come and visit me, and so they came, bringing their children and holding them up for me to see.

The Lebunge Ainos differ from the eastern Ainos. Their skin is very dark, their foreheads are low, their eyes are more deep-set, and they are shorter and hairier. These Ainos shave their hair two inches above their brows.

From their village, I began the longest stage of my journey, seventeen miles. **This path is so isolated that we didn't meet a single person on the road in four days of travel**. The Lebunge Valley is covered in thick forest and rocky ground. We continued over a narrow ridge, through bamboo forests, and through rugged ravines. We absolutely needed a guide, because **the trail disappeared at times**. But I have never seen grander forests than those.

By the time we got to Oshamambe, my spine was hurting so much that I had to stop for a day to rest.

しげで、さびれたところです。多くの人が何もせずにぶらぶらして、かなりの人が酒で酔っていました。

つぎに遊楽部へ向かいました。ここで、最後のアイヌ村を見かけました。海は明るい日差しを浴びて美しく、波が海岸に打ち寄せる音は、まるで音楽を奏でているようです。山越内という、海辺の小さな村のすてきな宿屋で1晩泊まったあと、森へと旅を続けました。ここで、アイヌのガイドから日本人のガイドに交代しました。森からの旅は、道がまったくないところがあったので、とてもたいへんでした。

その夜は峠下で泊まり、朝に目が覚めると、伊藤がわたしに尋ねました。「今朝が最後の朝になりますが、寂しくはありませんか？　わたしは寂しいです」。伊藤とわたしが何かについて同じ気持ちになったのは、とても久しぶりでした。わたしは蝦夷の旅が終わることと、とても役に立ってくれた賢い少年との別れが悲しくてなりませんでした。

とうとう函館に到着したとき、**外国人には誰にも出会いたくなかったのですが、そううまくはいきませんでした。**まずデニング氏と出会い、それから領事とヘプバーン博士に町で出会いました。わたしは路地に隠れようとしましたが、彼らがわたしを見つけて近づいてきたのです。とても恥ずかしい思いをしました。何日もの長旅のせいで泥だらけだったのですから！　まさに未開人のように見えたに違いありません。

Oshamambe looks sad and decaying. Many people lounge about doing nothing, and a good many were drunk from *sake*.

Next, we traveled to Yurapu. Here, we saw the last of the Aino villages. The ocean was beautiful in the bright sunlight, and the sound of the waves crashing on the shore was like booming music. After staying the night at a lovely *yadoya* in Yamakushinoi, a small hamlet on the seashore, we continued to Mori. This is where our Aino guide was replaced by a Japanese guide. Traveling from Mori was difficult, because in some parts there was no road or trail at all.

We stayed the night in Togenoshita, and when I woke in the morning, Ito asked me, "Are you sad that it's the last morning? I am." This was the first time in a while that Ito and I felt the same way about something. I was very sorry to end my Yezo tour and sorry to part with the clever boy who had made himself so useful to me.

When we finally arrived in Hakodate, I hoped **I would not run into any foreigners, but I had no luck**. First, I saw Mr. Dening, then the Consul and Dr. Hepburn saw me in town. I tried to hide down an alley but they saw me and approached. I was embarrassed because after many days of long travel, I was covered in mud! I'm sure I looked completely wild.

蝦夷、函館にて
1878年、9月14日

　今日が蝦夷での最後の日です。風の強い灰色の県庁所在地を照らす太陽は、駒ヶ岳の山頂をピンクと赤に染めています。この地の最後の印象は、最初のときと同じく輝かしいものです。湾は紺碧で、ところどころに紫色の陰があります。そこには、大きな白い帆を広げた60隻ほどの帆船が浮いています。江戸湾で初めて目にしたときと変わらないほど魅力的です。

　今日、ついに伊藤とお別れしました。とても悲しくて、すでに寂しくてたまりません。伊藤は忠実に仕えてくれて、とても多くのことを教えてくれました。彼はマリーズ氏のところへ行きました。マリーズ氏なら**強くて男らしい主人となって、伊藤がよい少年に育つよう導いてくれるでしょう**。それを思えば、うれしいことです。伊藤は出発するまえにも、室蘭の知事宛てに、人力車を使わせてくれたことや、その他の親切へのお礼の手紙を、わたしのために書いてくれました。

Hakodate, Yezo
September 14, 1878

This is my last day in Yezo. The sun, shining over this windy, grey capital is touching the peaks of Komono-taki with shades of pink and red. My last impressions of this place, like my first, are bright. The bay is deep blue sprinkled with violet shadows. There are about sixty junks floating on it with their great white sails. They are still as fascinating as when I saw them first in the Gulf of Yedo.

I finally parted with Ito today. It made me sad, and I miss him already. He served me faithfully, and he was a great source of information. He has gone to Mr. Maries, **who will be a strong, manly master and teach him to be a good boy**. I am glad of that. Before Ito left, he wrote a letter to the Governor of Mororan, thanking him on my behalf for the use of his *kuruma* and other courtesies.

江戸、英国公使館にて
9月21日

　兵庫丸に乗船したとき、海が穏やかで気圧も安定しているから、50時間という速さで横浜に到着するだろうとのことでした。**ところが航海に出ると突然台風に見舞われ、人生で最悪の船旅のひとつになったのです！**　台風、もしくは「回転するハリケーン」は25時間続き、ようやく横浜に着いたのは72時間後でした。上陸したのは17日の真夜中近くでしたが、もっとひどい災害を目にすることになりました。地域全体が洪水になり、首都への鉄道は止まり、暴動の噂まであったのです。人々は米の収穫のことを心配していました。そのうえ紙幣の価値が13パーセントも下がったのです！

　午後遅くに鉄道が再開したので、東京へ向かいました。東京の町は最高の眺めでした——屋敷は立派ですし、城の堀は蓮の花がいっぱいで、芝生は目にも鮮やかな緑です。今の東京は平和そうでした。暴動を率いた男たちは捕えられたのです。噂によれば、彼らは拷問され、そのうち52人は銃殺刑に処されたそうです。今年の夏はずっと天候不順でした。「きっと、そのうち変わるだろう」と人々は言います。でも、**わたしが5月にここへ着いたときにも、そう言っていたのです。**

H.B.M.'s Legation, Yedo
September 21

When I boarded the Hiogo Maru, the calm seas and steady barometer promised a quick fifty-hour trip to Yokohama. **However, when we got underway, we were hit by a sudden typhoon**, making the sea journey one of the worst in my life! The typhoon, or "revolving hurricane," lasted twenty-five hours, and we finally arrived in Yokohama after seventy-two hours. We landed near midnight on the 17th, only to find much disaster: the whole region was flooded, the railway to the capital was shut down, there were rumors of revolts. People were worried about the rice crop. The value of paper money was down 13 percent!

Late in the afternoon, the railroad was re-opened and I traveled to Tokiyo. The city is looking its best—its *yashikis* look handsome, the castle moat is filled with lotuses, and the grass is a brilliant green. Tokiyo seems peaceful now: the men who led a revolt were caught. People say they were tortured and fifty-two of them were shot. It has been a bad summer. "Surely, things will change soon," the people **say. But they were saying that when I arrived here in May.**

江戸、英国公使館にて
12月18日

　この10日間はこの地で夕食会へ行ったり、買い物をしたり、有名な池上寺や江の島、鎌倉へ行ったりして楽しく過ごしました。このようにいろいろなことをしましたが、ひとつの「名所」についてだけお話しましょう。それは桐ケ谷火葬場です。パークス卿が、そこを見学する許可を申請してくださいました。そして数日後、知事本人から許可をいただいたのです。わたしは知事に会いに、彼の立派な屋敷へ行きました。

　知事の楠本氏は育ちのよい人で、たいへん有能です。彼は北日本での旅について尋ね、率直な意見を聞きたいと言われました。とはいえ、**東洋ではこういう要求を文字どおりとらないほうがいい**と知っているので、道路事情が悪いとだけ答えました。

　楠本氏は、自分の通訳と人力車を使って目黒へ行くようにと言われました。そこでわたしたちは人力車に1時間乗って、赤い椿や竹でいっぱいの山や谷のある、少し郊外のほうへ向かいました。やがて煙突と高い屋根のある小さな灰色の建物に着きました。これが火葬場です。

　小さな寺もあり、仏像や赤い骨壺がぎっしりと並んで売られています。その向こうに、土間と土壁の部屋が4つあり、どの部屋もじつに清潔で、とくに目を引くものはあり

H.B.M.'s Legation, Yedo
December 18

I've spent the last ten days here pleasantly, going to dinner parties, shopping, and making excursions to the famous temples of Ikegami, to Enoshima and to Kamakura. Of all these various activities, I will mention only one "sight": the cremation grounds of Kirigaya. Sir Parkes applied for permission for me to see it. A few days later, permission was granted from the Governor himself. I went to see him at his fine *yashiki*.

Mr. Kusamoto, the Governor, is a well-bred man, and very capable. He asked me about my travels in the north and asked for my honest criticism. I know, however, that **in the east one should not take this request literally**, so I simply said the roads were in a bad state.

Mr. Kusamoto invited me to use his own interpreter and carriage to go to Meguro. So we drove for an hour to a little suburb of hills and valleys full of red camellias and bamboo. We came to a little grey building with chimneys and a high roof. This was the crematorium.

There was also a little temple crowded with religious images and red urns for sale. Beyond this were four rooms with earthen floors and walls, all

ません。部屋はがらんとしていて、数対の石の台があるだけです。一番大きな部屋では、数体の遺体を一度に焼くことができ、費用は1円しかかかりません。

葬式のあと、遺体はここへ運ばれます。大きな部屋には5つの「桶」があって、使用人や貧しい労働者の遺体が入っています。小さな部屋には、中流階級の人の遺体が入った長方形の松の箱があります。午後8時に、それぞれの棺は石の台に置かれ、その下で火がつけられます。午前6時までに、遺体は小さな灰の山になります。これは骨箱に納められて、遺族に渡されます。遺族はその骨壺を土のなかに埋葬しますが、そのとき僧侶に来てもらうこともあります。

わたしが訪れたまえの日に、13体の遺体が焼かれました。その全工程がとても清潔なので驚きました。臭いはまったくありません。その簡素さは目を見張るもので、**じつに効果的で安価な遺体の処理方法なのは間違いありません。**

気船ヴォルガにて、1878年、クリスマス・イブ——雪で覆われた富士山の頂が、ミシシッピ湾【編注：根岸湾】を囲む森の上で朝日に赤く染まるなか、わたしたちは19日に横浜港を出航しました。その3日後、日本の姿を目にするのも最後となりました。それは、海の波に洗われる岩だらけの海岸でした。

東海道の村から見た富士山
Fujisan, from a Village on the Tokaido

very clean and unremarkable. The rooms were empty except for several pairs of stone supports. In the largest room, several bodies are burned at a time, and the cost is only one yen.

After the funeral service, the body is brought here. There are five "tubs" in the large room containing the bodies of servants and poor laborers. In the small rooms, there are long pine boxes containing the bodies of middle-class people. At 8 p.m., each coffin is placed on the stone supports, and a fire is lit underneath it. By 6 a.m., the body has become a little pile of ashes. This is placed in an urn and given to the mourning family. The family then buries the urn, sometimes with a priest attending.

Thirteen bodies were burned the night before my visit. It was surprising how clean the whole process was. There was absolutely no smell. The simplicity of it all is remarkable, and **there's no doubt it is a very effective and cheap way to destroy corpses**.

S.S. Volga, Christmas Eve, 1878—The snow-covered top of Fujisan was turning red in the sunrise above the surrounding forests of Mississippi Bay when we steamed out of Yokohama Harbor on the 19th. Three days later, I had my last glimpse of Japan: a rugged coast being beaten by the sea.

[対訳ニッポン双書]
日本奥地紀行(縮約版)
Unbeaten Tracks in Japan

2017年4月5日　第1刷発行

原 著 者　イザベラ・バード

英文リライト　ニーナ・ウェグナー

翻　　訳　牛原　眞弓

発行者　浦　　晋　亮

発行所　IBCパブリッシング株式会社
　　　　〒162-0804 東京都新宿区中里町29番3号 菱秀神楽坂ビル9F
　　　　Tel. 03-3513-4511 Fax. 03-3513-4512
　　　　www.ibcpub.co.jp

印刷所　中央精版印刷株式会社

© IBC パブリッシング 2017
Printed in Japan

落丁本・乱丁本は、小社宛にお送りください。送料小社負担にてお取り替えいたします。
本書の無断複写(コピー)は著作権法上での例外を除き禁じられています。

ISBN978-4-7946-0471-2